Contents

Introduction

INTRODUCTION

This revised edition of A Guide to Housing Rights, written in the context of a severe recession, is a comprehensive overview of housing across all tenures and is aimed specifically at the layperson, although it can be utilised by the professional.

Housing is very complex and affects all people at some point in their lives. Housing law is ever changing and knowledge of it is usually outside the scope of the layperson. Specialist workers and advisers are needed to make sense of the maze. There is the problem of homelessness and what to do at this traumatic time. How do local authorities work and what are their obligations towards the individual? What is the role of housing associations and housing co-operatives and how can one gain access to this type of property?

In addition, what happens if a person is subject to domestic violence and flees home? What are the obligations of local authorities and housing associations at this time? What happens if a relationship breaks down, what are the rights and obligations of the respective parties at a time like this?

A Guide to Housing Rights covers all areas in relation to housing. The rights of the private tenant are covered in depth, along with the rights and obligations of the public sector tenant.

Owner occupation is also covered in depth, in particular the rights and obligations of the leaseholder. The roles of intermediaries are covered along with mortgages and other aspects of owning a home.

A Guide to Housing Rights is an extremely comprehensive guide to all aspects of housing and should prove invaluable to all.

Roger Sproston

1

HOUSING RIGHTS GENERALLY

Whether to rent or buy

Although we have witnessed a prolonged period of falling house prices, after the boom of the last thirty years,, buying a home in most areas is still only an option for those who can afford the prices and get a mortgage. We are in a market where the majority of first time buyers are still excluded from buying a home. There are advantages to buying a property, if you can. They are as follows:

- When buying you will have a wider choice of property and areas, obviously depending on the price range you can afford.
- You will have more control over your home than when renting.
- You can only normally lose your home if you do not keep up your mortgage repayments.
- In the longer term, it can be cheaper than renting and over the years you will build up equity in the property until you eventually own it.

There are disadvantages to owning, as follows:
- The costs in the early years are usually higher than renting a property, particularly from a local authority or housing association, although usually lower than the private sector.
- There is an initial high cost to buying a house, whereas this is not the case with rented property.
- As an owner-occupier you will be responsible for all repairs and maintenance which can be expensive.

- There is very limited help with your housing costs if your income drops.

Obviously, the ideal landlord from whom to rent is a local authority or a housing association. The advantages of this are:

- Costs are usually lower than the private sector and rents are regulated. However, rents have climbed, particularly in the Housing Association sector following changes to rent setting since 2011.
- If your income drops you are usually eligible for housing benefit although there have been significant changes to benefit entitlement since April 2013.
- Most of the repairs and maintenance will be carried out by the landlord, from rental income.
- You will only lose your home if you breach the terms of the tenancy agreement.
- The public sector is non-profit making and will usually be good landlords.

There are disadvantages to renting from a local authority or housing association:

- In some areas there is a very long waiting list for properties. When you eventually are housed it may not be in an area of choice.
- The rent will gradually increase, reaching levels higher than those who own and you will not build up any equity in your property.

Private landlords have increased greatly over the last 15 years, particularly with the advent of buy-to-let, although this sector experienced a slow-down it is once again on the ascent. There are some advantages to renting from a private landlord. They are:

- There will be a wider choice of areas and properties than in the public sector, if you have the means to rent them.
- There is rarely a waiting list.
- You can get help with your rent if your income drops. Most of the repairs and maintenance will be met by the landlord out of rent.

There are, as always, disadvantages to renting in the private sector:

- Rents can be very high. This is the case particularly in the south east.
- Rent will go up over time, usually more than the public sector.
- Tenants in the private sector have limited protection. In the public sector, tenancies are usually for life, subject to breach of contract. Homeowners own the property they live in. Private sector tenants are in the weakest position. With six-month tenancies being the norm.

Different types of house and tenancy will suit different people at different times of their lives, depending on their circumstances. There are many things to consider when making a decision, these being outlined below.

Renting from a local authority

Council homes are, along with housing association property and, in some cases, housing co-operatives, the most affordable type of housing. However, they are also the most difficult to obtain. The allocation of council housing will depend on your need and those in the most need will usually be given priority over others. This has been a bone of contention for many years, however, need is measured in a scientific way, with points allocated according to different circumstances. Most local authorities run a bidding system which has made it more difficult for people to both obtain or swap housing.

You can find out from the council housing department about how to go about making an application for housing. If you are being actively considered for an offer of housing then the council will usually send someone to visit you. In most cases, it is necessary to reregister on the housing register each year, in order to keep an active list of those in need.

The housing register

Councils will keep a list, or register of people who apply for housing. This has been a requirement for some years now. This register is also sometimes known as a 'waiting list' although this is misleading since length of time on the list is certainly not the only factor taken into account when it comes to being rehoused. In the main, councils now operate a list where people bid for housing in an area.

A council can decide that a person is not eligible for housing if they have been guilty of behaviour that would entitle them to evict that person as a council tenant.

People arriving from abroad

Some people from abroad are not allowed to register on the housing list. This includes people who are subject to immigration control, people who are allowed to stay subject to not benefiting from public funds and sponsored immigrants who have been in the United Kingdom for less than five years. Also, people who fail the habitual residence test for welfare benefits or who are in breach of EU Rights of Residence Directive. If a local authority refuses to put your name on the housing register, you have the right to ask them to review their decision within 21 days. There are special arrangements for asylum seekers who will be directed towards accommodation in limited areas of the country.

Homelessness

Local authorities have a legal duty to provide help to certain people who are homeless or threatened with homelessness. You will qualify for help if you are 'eligible for assistance', legally homeless or threatened with homelessness and not intentionally homeless. In England, Wales and Northern Ireland, you must also be in priority need. This test was abolished in Scotland on 31 December 2012. The local authority may also investigate whether you have a local connection with the area.

Local social services authorities also have responsibility for some homeless people. They have a duty to provide accommodation for children and young people over 16 who are leaving care, or who are in need for other reasons.

Local authorities must not discriminate against you. For example, if you don't understand English, the local authority should provide help and information in your own language

Eligible for Assistance

Certain people who arrive in this country, or who are returning from a period living abroad do not qualify for housing under homelessness laws. For example, many asylum-seekers (but not all) are excluded, as is someone who has spent significant time living away from the UK even if they are a UK citizen. The rules on eligibility are complex and if you are arriving in or returning to the UK, you should seek specialist advice at, for example, at a Citizens Advice Bureau.

Homelessness or threatened with homelessness

You will be considered legally homeless if you have no accommodation which is available and reasonable for you and your household to live in. This includes accommodation in another country. You will also be homeless if you have accommodation but cannot get into it. For example, if you have somewhere to stay with friends or relatives but have been asked to leave, or you are at risk of violence in your home. You will be considered to be threatened with homelessness, if you are likely to be homeless within 28 days (in Scotland, two months).

Priority need

You will be counted as having a 'priority need' for housing if you are homeless and:

- you are pregnant
- you have dependent children under 16, or under 19 if they are in full-time education
- you are homeless because of an emergency such as a flood or a fire
- you are aged 16 or 17.

You may also be in priority need if you fall into one of the following groups. In some cases, you may have to show that your situation has made you vulnerable:-

- you are elderly, or have a physical or mental illness or disability
- you are over 18 but at risk of exploitation or have been in care
- you are at risk of domestic violence, racial violence or other threats of violence
- you are homeless after leaving hospital, prison or the armed forces.

The groups of people who have a priority need are different depending on whether you live in England, Wales or Northern Ireland, or in Scotland before the test was abolished.. If you think you fall into a priority need group you can check this with a specialist adviser, for example, at a Citizens Advice Bureau.

Intentionally homeless

You may be considered 'intentionally homeless' if you have deliberately done something which has made you lose your home. However, the definition of intentionally homeless is complicated and a decision made by your local authority can often be successfully challenged. For example, if you have become homeless because of rent or mortgage arrears you should not automatically be considered to be intentionally homeless. The local authority must look at each case individually. If you lost your home because of genuine financial problems you will not be homeless through your own fault.

Priority need

The local authority may refuse to accept responsibility if it thinks that you have no connection with the area where you are looking for help with housing. You would usually be expected to live, work or have family links to have a local connection. In this situation, you may be referred to an area where you do have a connection.

What action must the local authority take?

If the local authority needs time to carry out enquiries (and if it seems that you are homeless and, in England, Wales and Northern Ireland, in priority need), it must make sure you have somewhere to live while it investigates your situation.

If you qualify as homeless, the local authority will have to help you. It does not have to provide accommodation from its own properties. It can house you in various ways, for example, by referring you to a housing association, or arranging accommodation with a private landlord.

If the local authority decides that you are not homeless, it does not have any duties to arrange long-term accommodation for you. However, it will have some duties to help you, and must provide advice and assistance in finding accommodation, or provide a temporary place to stay while you find a permanent home.

The local authority must give reasons for its decision if it decides you aren't homeless and tell you about the right to review a decision, or appeal it, if you live in Northern Ireland.

Other rights to re-housing

People who lose their homes as a result of action by the local authority will, usually, have a right to re-housing. Councils may make a compulsory purchase order on a house and then demolish it, councils may decide that a property needs improving and occupiers have to move out permanently. If this is the case then there is a right to re-housing. Anyone legally living in the property at the time of these actions is entitled to re-housing, the right applying to owners or tenants. It does not apply to those moving in after the action has commenced or to squatters.

People who have to vacate their homes in these circumstances can also claim home loss payment to a maximum of £15,000, (check current figures with your local authority as they are subject to change) disturbance payment to help with the costs of moving and a well-maintained payment which involves a payment to the owners or tenants if the property is to be compulsory purchased and has been well maintained up to the time of compulsory purchase.

Other council housing schemes in operation

In addition to those schemes outlined above, councils have a number of other schemes in operation. The most common area:

Hard-to-let or low-demand schemes. This is where the council has unpopular homes in areas that are blighted for example, or in tower blocks. Property like this is typically offered to low priority groups such as young single people.

Schemes for special groups-Some council's have quotas for special groups, such as for those with special needs, mental illness etc.

Exchanging properties

Tenants of public sector housing, at least secure and assured tenants, have the right to exchange their homes with another person or family, subject to permission from the landlord, which cannot be unreasonably withheld. There are a number of reasons why the council or association can refuse to let an exchange go ahead:

- There is a court order to evict one of the applicants
- There is impending possession proceedings
- The accommodation you want to transfer is larger than your needs (substantially larger)
- The accommodation is too small
- The landlord is a charity and the proposed new tenant does not suit the aims and objectives of the landlord
- Accommodation is specially adapted for a person with physical disabilities and the proposed new tenant is not disabled.
- The accommodation is managed by a tenant management co-operative and the proposed tenant does not want to become part of the co-operative.

Housing associations

Housing associations and housing trusts are slightly different to councils in their make up. Although publicly funded and accountable to a board of management and to the Tenant Services Authority, which is a quango set up by Parliament to regulate the activities of associations, they are more independent than councils.

Housing associations will offer a variety of tenancy types, some not offered by councils. However, they will work closely with the local authority when it comes to receiving nominations and referrals for housing. Often, they are only permitted to develop in a local authority area if they agree an ongoing quota of nominations from councils. Many associations will only house those on the housing register. However, if you have a problem getting onto the housing register then you should seek advice form the council.

Housing associations which are registered with the TSA are obliged by law to give details of how they allocate tenancies. Some associations will take direct applications others will work through agencies. It depends on the associations.

Housing association tenancies are usually assured and assured shorthold, with some secure, usually created out of an exchange. However, as we will see a little later, housing associations have not been able to grant secure tenancies since January 1st 1989 and therefore, the secure tenancy, which is now a local authority tenancy only, is dwindling in associations.

Renting from a private landlord

If you cannot afford to buy a property, as a lot of people cannot due to rising house prices, and you do not qualify for a council or housing association tenancy then you will need to do as a growing number of people do, and that is rent from a private landlord. This is usually the most expensive way of renting but there is usually availability of property.

The majority of private lets are found through local estate agents with a letting arm. They will advertise property and vet prospective tenants, taking up references and also provide a management service to the landlord that can cost anything between 10-15% of rental income plus VAT. Many agencies will charge the tenant a fee for drawing up a tenancy but are not allowed to charge a deposit before a property is found. On finding a property you will need to pay a deposit which is returnable. The deposit is now protected by the Tenancy Deposit Protection Scheme, introduced in 2007. Renting a property is outlined in more depth further on in the book.

Housing co-operatives

Housing co-operatives consist of groups of people who each have a share in the overall co-op, usually a £1 share and each have a responsibility for managing the co-op, usually delegated to a committee. Individuals are expected to show an active interest and participate in the day-to-day running. Co-ops will allocate their own property but will also sometimes have agreements with local authorities. Three are relatively few co-ops in existence and they are difficult to get into.

2

The Law and Mobile Homes

If you own a mobile home, rent a pitch for it on a site and use it as your main residence, you will be protected by the Mobile Homes Act 1983 as amended by the Housing Act 2004. If you rent the home you will be covered by the law for tenants. The Act does not cover you if you only rent the home for holidays.

Protection from eviction

The Mobile Homes Act 1983, as amended by the Housing Act 2004, gives owners the right to keep their homes on the site they occupy indefinitely. There can only be a fixed time limit on the agreement if the site owner's planning permission, or right to use the land, is itself limited to a fixed period. If the time limit is later extended, then so is your right to stay there. The resident can bring the agreement to an end by giving at least four weeks notice in writing. The site owner can only bring the agreement to an end by applying to the county court or to an arbitrator. There are only three grounds on which the site owner can seek to end an agreement:

- You are not living in the mobile home as your main residence.
- The mobile home is having a detrimental effect on the site because of its age or condition or is likely to have this effect within the next five years. The site owner can only try to use this ground for ending the agreement once in any five-year period, starting from the date the agreement began.
- You have broken one of the terms of the agreement and the court or the arbitrator thinks it is reasonable to end the agreement. The site owner must first tell you that you have

broken the agreement and give you a reasonable time to put things right.

If the site owner can prove to the court or the arbitrator that the agreement should be brought to an end for one of these reasons, the site owner can then get an eviction order from the courts. Arbitrators cannot make eviction orders. The site owner can normally go to court to end the agreement and for an eviction order at the same time.

If the site is privately owned, the court can suspend an eviction order for up to one year, but cannot suspend it if the site is owned by the local council. It is a criminal offence for the site owner to evict you without a court order, to harass or threaten you or to cut off services such as gas, electricity or water in order to get you to leave.

The site owner can only make you move to another part of the site if:

- Your agreement says that this can be done
- The new pitch is broadly comparable to the old one
- The site owner pays all the costs.

The right to a written agreement and a statement of rights

The site owner must give you a statement of your legal rights and the terms of your agreement. The agreement cannot change your rights under the Mobile Homes Act. You or the site owner can apply to change the terms of the agreement within six months of the issue of the original agreement. Either side can apply to the county court or an arbitrator, if they cannot agree the terms. You should always check the agreement for the terms of payment and fees and if not happy apply to change them.

Other rights of mobile home owners

You can sell your home and pass on the agreement with the site owner to a person of your choice. You can also give your home to a member of your family. In either case, the new owner must be approved by the site owner, but this approval cannot be unreasonably withheld. If this is the case then you can apply to the county court or an arbitrator for an order for the site owner to give approval. If you sell your home the site owner can claim a commission of up to 20% of the price. If you die members of your family who were living with you will automatically inherit the agreement with the site owner and your legal rights.

New legislation
New legislation is coming into force in 2013 to protect the rights of mobile home owners.

The Mobile Homes Bill, having been approved by both Houses of Parliament, received Royal Assent on 26 March and the sections of the Mobile Homes Act 2013 will start coming into force on 26 May 2013. Sections 1 – 7, which deal with the changes to the licensing regime, will come into force on 1 April 2014. Sections 9 – 12 which deal with park rules, the removal of the requirement to obtain the park owner's consent to a prospective purchaser or person being gifted a home, and pitch fee reviews come into force on 26 May 2013. The other sections, including the much discussed fit and proper person test will not come into force until a statutory instrument to that effect has been made.

3

PRIVATE TENANTS
FINDING A PROPERTY

Letting Agents

When looking for a property, there are obvious advantages in using an agent: they are likely to be experienced, can provide you with a tenancy agreement and they can provide a service after the property is let. It is important for a tenant to know that there will be a proper relationship between him/her and the landlord after moving in. Managing agents will provide this link.

Agents will typically look after the following:

- Transfer the utility bills and the council tax into the name of the tenant.
- Pay for repairs, although an agent will only normally do this if rent is being paid directly to them and they can make appropriate deductions.
- Chase rent arrears
- Serve notices of intent to seek possession if the landlord instructs them to do. An agent cannot commence court proceedings except through a solicitor.
- Visit the property at regular intervals check that the tenants are not causing any damage.
- Deal with neighbour complaints
- Bank rental receipts if the landlord is abroad

- Deal with housing benefit departments if necessary.

The extent to which agents actually do any or all of the following really depends on the calibre of the agent. It also depends on the type of agreement the landlord has with the agent.

Beware! There are many rental agencies. These agents are not all professional, many do not know a thing about property management and are shady and should be avoided like the plague. Shop around and seek a reputable agent. Beware also of charges levied by agents. they can vary wildly, especially in London where demand has exceeded supply and agents and landlords can tend to be predatory and unscrupulous.

Advertisements

The classified advertisement section of local papers is a good place to seek a property. Local papers are obviously cheaper than the nationals such as the Evening Standard in London or the broadsheets such as the Guardian. The type of newspaper you look in will largely reflect what type of property you are looking for. An advert in the pages of the Times would indicate that the landlord is looking for a well-heeled professional and this would be reflected in the type of property that is to let.

Company lets

Where the tenant is a company rather than an individual, the tenancy agreement will be similar to an assured shorthold, but will not be bound by the six-month rule (see chapter 7 for details of assured shorthold tenancies). Company lets can be from any length of time, from a week to several years, or as long as you like.

The major difference between contracts and standard assured shorthold agreements is that the contract will be tailored to individual needs, and the agreement is bound by the provisions of contract law. Company tenancies are bound by the provisions of contract law and not by the 1988 Housing

Act. Note: if you are a company and you are looking for a property to rent let you must use a letting agent or solicitor. Most landlords will insist on it.

The advantages of a landlord letting to a company are:

- A company or embassy has no security of tenure and therefore cannot be a sitting tenant.
- A company cannot seek to reduce the rent by statutory interventions.
- Rental payments are often made quarterly or six monthly in advance.
- The financial status of a company is usually more secure than that of an individual.
- Company tenants often require long-term lets to accommodate staff relocating on contracts of between one and five years.

The main disadvantages of company lets are:

- A company tenancy can only be to a bona fide company or embassy, not to a private individual.
- A tenancy to a partnership would not count as a company let and may have some security of tenure.
- If the tenant is a foreign government, the diplomatic status of the occupant must be ascertained, as the courts cannot enforce breaches of contract with somebody who possesses diplomatic immunity.
- A tenancy to a foreign company not registered in the U.K may prove time consuming and costly if it becomes necessary to pursue claims for unpaid rent or damage through foreign courts.

Short-lets

Although company lets can be of any length, it is becoming increasingly popular for companies to rent flats from private landlords on short-lets.

A short let is any let of less than six months. But here, it is essential to check the rules with the local authority concerned. Some boroughs will not allow lets for less than three months, as they do not want to encourage transient people in the neighbourhood.

Generally speaking, short-lets are only applicable in large cities where there is a substantial shifting population. Business executives on temporary relocation, actors and others involved in television production or film work, contract workers and visiting academics are examples of people who might require a short-let.

From a landlord's point of view, short-lets are an excellent idea if you have to vacate your own home for seven or eight months, say, and do not want to leave it empty for that time. Short-let tenants provide useful extra income as well as keeping an eye on the place. Or, if you are buying a new property and have not yet sold the old one, it can make good business sense to let it to a short-let tenant.

Short-let tenants are, usually, from a landlord's point of view, excellent blue-chip occupants. They are busy professionals, high earners, out all day and used to high standards. As the rent is paid by the company there is no worry for the landlord on this score either.

A major plus of short-lets is that they command between 20-50% more rent than the optimum market rent for that type of property. The one downside of short-lets is that no agency can guarantee permanent occupancy.

Student lets

Many letting agencies will not consider students and a lot of landlords similarly are not keen. There is the perception that students will not look after a home and tend to live a lifestyle guaranteed to increase the wear and tear on a property. However, if handled correctly, student lets can be profitable. Although students quite often want property for only eight or nine months, agencies that deal with students make them sign for a whole year. Rent is guaranteed by confirmation that the student is a genuine student with references from parents, who act as guarantors.

There can be a lot of money made from student lets. However, the tenancy will require more avid policing because of the nature of student lifestyle.

The DSS and housing benefit

Very few letting agencies or landlords will touch DSS or housing benefits tenants. However, as with student lets, there is another side of the coin.

Quite often it is essential for a tenant on HB to have a guarantor, usually a homeowner, before signing a tenancy. Then it is up to the machinations of the benefit system to ensure that the landlord receives rent. The rent is assessed by a benefit officer, with the rent estimated usually at market price. There are rent levels set for each are that the benefit officer will not go above.

A deposit is paid normally and rent is usually paid direct to the landlord. However, sweeping changes to benefit rules in 2013, with the introduction of Universal Credit, plus the requirement that rent is paid direct to the tenant have made landlords more wary of accepting tenants on benefits..

Although tenants on HB have a bad name, due to stereotyping, there are many reasons why a person may be on benefit and probably does not fit the picture of a scrounger who will trash a property. If housing benefit tenancies are managed well, then this can be a useful source of tenant.

Holiday-lets

Before the Housing Act 1988 became law, many landlords advertised their properties as holiday-lets to bypass the rules regarding security of tenure. Strictly speaking, a holiday-let is a property let for no more than a month to any one tenant. If the same tenant renews for another month then the landlord is breaking the law. Nowadays, holiday-lets must be just that-let for a genuine holiday.

Holiday-lets are not covered by the Housing Act. The contract is finalized by exchange of letters with the tenant where they place a deposit and the owner confirms the booking. If the let is not for a genuine holiday you may have problems in evicting the tenant, as the whole point of a holiday let is that it is for no more than a fixed period of a month.

Generally speaking, certain services must be provided for the let to be deemed a holiday-let. Cleaning services and changes of bed linen are essential. The amount paid by the holidaymaker will usually include utilities but would exclude use of the telephone, fax machine etc.

If possible, you should talk to someone with some experience of this type of let before entering into an agreement with an agency. The usual problems may arise, those of ensuring occupancy all year round and the maintenance of your property, which will be higher due to a high turnover.

Bed-sits

Bed-sitting rooms are usually difficult to let and can cause problems for tenants as well as landlords. It is best to leave this area of letting alone. There are numerous regulations to adhere to, Houses in Multiple Occupation regulations are quite strict. There is a problem also of high turnover. Leave this kind of letting to others and concentrate on houses or flats.

Viewing a property

Once you have found a property, the next stage is to make arrangements for a viewing. It is a good idea to make all appointments on the same day in order to avoid wasting time. If you decide on a likely property, the landlord will wish to take up references, if an agency is not being used. This will normally be a previous landlord's reference and also a bank reference. Only when these have been received and it is established that the person(s) are safe will the letting go ahead. No keys will be handed over until the cheque has been cleared and the landlord is in receipt of a month's rent and a month's deposit.

Deposits

Tenancy Deposit Protection Scheme

The Tenancy Deposit Protection Scheme was introduced to protect all deposits paid to landlords after 6th April 2007. After this date, landlords and/or agents must use a government authorised scheme to protect deposits. The need for such a scheme has arisen because of the historical problem with deposits and the abuse of deposits by landlords.

The scheme works as follows:
Moving into a property

At the beginning of a new tenancy agreement, the tenant will pay a deposit to the landlord or agent as usual. Within 14 days the landlord is required to give 30 the tenant details of how the deposit is going to be protected including:

- the contact details of the tenancy deposit scheme
- the contact details of landlord or agent
- how to apply for the release of the deposit
- what to do if there is a dispute about the deposit

There are three tenancy deposit schemes that a landlord can opt for:

25

Tenancy Deposit Solutions Ltd
www.mydeosits.co.uk
info@mydeposits.co.uk

The Tenancy Deposit Scheme
www.tds.gb.com
0845 226 7837

The Deposit Protection Service
www.depositprotection.com
0870 707 1 707

The schemes above fall into two categories, insurance based schemes and custodial schemes.

Custodial Scheme

- The tenant pays the deposit to the landlord
- The landlord pays the deposit into the scheme
- Within 14 days of receiving the deposit, the landlord must give the tenant prescribed information
- A the end of the tenancy, if the landlord and tenant have agreed how much of the deposit is to be returned, they will tell the scheme which returns the deposit, divided in the way agreed by the parties.
- If there is a dispute, the scheme will hold the disputed amount until the dispute resolution service or courts decide what is fair
- The interest accrued by deposits in the scheme will be used to pay for the running of the scheme and any surplus will be used to offer interest to the tenant, or landlord if the tenant isn't entitled to it.

Insurance based schemes

- The tenant pays the deposit to the landlord
- The landlord retains the deposit and pays a premium to the insurer (this is the key difference between the two schemes)
- Within 14 days of receiving a deposit the landlord must give the tenant prescribed information.
- At the end of the tenancy if the landlord and tenant agree how the deposit is to be divided or otherwise then the landlord will return the amount agreed
- If there is a dispute, the landlord must hand over the disputed amount to the scheme for safekeeping until the dispute is resolved
- If for any reason the landlord fails to comply, the insurance arrangements will ensure the return of the deposit to the tenant if they are entitled to it.

If a landlord or agent hasn't protected a deposit with one of the above then the tenant can apply to the local county court for an order for the landlord either to protect the deposit or repay it.

Rental guarantees

The landlord will always obtain a guarantor if there is any potential uncertainty as to payment of rent. One example is where the tenant is on benefits. The guarantor will be expected to assume responsibility for the rent if the tenant ceases to pay at any time during the term of the tenancy.

Moving out

At the end of the tenancy, check whether you are leaving the property in good order. Allow for fair wear and tear if the condition has deteriorated because of your use. Agree with your landlord how much of the deposit should be returned and within ten days the balance of the deposit or the entire deposit if appropriate will be returned to you.

Resolving disputes

When you move out, if there is a dispute then there will be a free service offered by the elected scheme to help resolve the dispute. It is important to remember that until the dispute is resolved then the deposit will be held by the scheme. It is also important to understand that the landlord cannot give you notice to end the tenancy until he or she has protected the deposit and given you notice as to how it is going to be protected.

For information generally about Tenancy Deposit protection you should visit www.tenancydeposit.gov.uk.

This site will tell you in detail how the whole scheme works.

4

PRIVATE TENANTS AND THE LAW

Explaining the law

As a tenant, or potential tenant, it is very important to understand the rights and obligations of both yourself and your landlord, exactly what can and what cannot be done once the tenancy agreement has been signed and you have moved into the property.

Some landlords think they can do exactly as they please, because the property belongs to them. Some tenants do not know any differently and therefore the landlord can, and often does, get away with breaking the law. However, this is not the case, there is a very strong legal framework governing the relationship between landlord and tenant and it is important that you have a grasp on the key principles of the law.

In order to fully understand the law we should begin by looking at the main types of relationship between people and their homes.

The freehold and the lease

In law, there are two main types of ownership and occupation of property. These are: freehold and leasehold. These arrangements are very old indeed.

Freehold

If a person owns their property outright (usually with a mortgage) then they are a freeholder. The only claims to ownership over and above their own might be those of the building society or the bank, which lent them the money to buy the place. They will re-possess the property if the mortgage payments are not kept up with.

In certain situations though, the local authority (council) for an area can affect a person's right to do what they please with their home even if they are a freeholder. This will occur when planning powers are exercised, for example, in order to prevent the carrying out of alterations without consent.

The local authority for your area has many powers and we will be referring to these regularly.

Leasehold

If a person lives in a property owned by someone else and has a written agreement allowing them to occupy the flat or house for a period of time i.e., giving them permission to live in that property, then they will, in the main, have a lease and either be a leaseholder or a tenant of a landlord.

The main principle of a lease is that a person has been given permission by someone else to live in his or her property for a period of time. The person giving permission could be either the freeholder or another leaseholder.

The tenancy agreement is one type of lease. If you have signed a tenancy agreement then you will have been given permission by a person to live in their property for a period of time.

The position of the tenant

The tenant will usually have an agreement for a shorter period of time than the typical leaseholder. Whereas the leaseholder will, for example, have an agreement for ninety-nine years, the tenant will have an agreement, which either runs from week to week or month to month (periodic tenancy) or is for a fixed term, for example, six-months or one-year.

These arrangements are the most common types of agreement between the private landlord and tenant.

The agreement itself will state whether it is a fixed-term or periodic tenancy. If an agreement has not been issued it will be assumed to be a fixed term tenancy.

Both periodic and fixed-term tenants will usually pay a sum of rent regularly to a landlord in return for permission to live in the property (more about rent and service charges later)

The tenancy agreement

The tenancy agreement is the usual arrangement under which one person will live in a property owned by another. Before a tenant moves into a property he/she will have to sign a tenancy agreement drawn up by a landlord or landlord's agent. *A tenancy agreement is a contract between landlord and tenant.*

It is important to realize that when you sign a tenancy agreement, you have signed a contract with another person, which governs the way in which you will live in their property.

The contract

Typically, any tenancy agreement will show the name and address of the landlord and will state the names of the tenant(s). The type of tenancy agreement that is signed should be clearly indicated. This could be, for example, a Rent Act protected tenancy, an assured tenancy or an assured shorthold tenancy. In the main, in the private sector, the agreement will be an assured shorthold.

Date of commencement of tenancy and rent payable

The date the tenancy began and the duration (fixed term or periodic) plus the amount of rent payable should be clearly shown, along with who is responsible for any other charges, such as water rates, council tax etc, and a description of the property you are living in. The landlord must also serve a notice stating the address to where any legal notices can be sent.

In addition to the rent that must be paid there should be a clear indication of when a rent increase can be expected. This information is sometimes shown in other conditions of tenancy, which should be given to the tenant when they move into their home. The conditions of tenancy will set out landlords and tenants rights and obligations.

Services provided under the tenancy and service of notice

If services are provided, i.e., if a service charge is payable, this should be indicated in the agreement. The tenancy agreement, as stated, should indicate clearly the address to which notices on the landlord can be served by the tenant, for example, because of repair problems or notice of leaving the property. The landlord has a legal requirement to indicate this.

Tenants obligations

The tenancy agreement will either be a basic document with the above information or will be more comprehensive. Either way, there will be a section beginning "the tenant agrees." Here the tenant will agree to move into the property, pay rent, use the property as an only home, not cause a nuisance to others, take responsibility for certain internal repairs, not sublet the property, i.e., create another tenancy, and various other things depending on the property.

Landlords obligations

There should also be another section "the landlord agrees". Here, the landlord is contracting with the tenant to allow quiet enjoyment of the property. The landlord's repairing responsibilities are also usually outlined.

Ending a tenancy

Finally, there should be a section entitled "ending the tenancy" which will outline the ways in which landlord and tenant can end the agreement. It is in this section that the landlord should make reference to the "grounds for possession". Grounds for possession are circumstances where the landlord will apply to court for possession of his/her property. Some of these grounds relate to what is in the tenancy, i.e., the responsibility to pay rent and to not cause a nuisance. Other grounds do not relate to the contents of the tenancy directly, but more to the law governing that particular tenancy. The grounds for possession are very important, as they are used in any court case brought against the tenant. Unfortunately, they are not always indicated in the tenancy agreement. As they are so important they are summarized later on in this chapter.

It must be said at this point that many residential tenancies are very light on landlord's responsibilities. Repairing responsibilities, and responsibilities relating to rental payment, are landlord's obligations under law. This book deals with these, and other areas. However, many landlords will seek to use only the most basic document in order to conceal legal obligations.

The public sector tenancy (local authority or housing association), for example, is usually very clear and very comprehensive about the rights and obligations of landlord and tenant. Unfortunately, the private landlord often does not employ the same energy when it comes to educating and informing the tenant.

The responsibility of the landlord to provide a tenant with a rent book

If the tenant is a weekly periodic tenant the landlord must provide him/her with a rent book and commits a criminal offence if he/she does not do so. This is outlined in the Landlord and Tenant Act 1985 sections 4 - 7. Under this Act any tenant can ask in writing the name and address of the landlord.
The landlord must reply within twenty-one days of asking.

As most tenancies nowadays are fixed term assured shortholds then it is not strictly necessary to provide a tenant with a rent book. However, for the purposes of efficiency, and your own records, it is always useful to have a rent book and sign it each time rent is collected or a standing order is paid.

Overcrowding and the rules governing too many people living in the property

It is important to understand, when signing a tenancy agreement, that it is not permitted to allow the premises to become overcrowded, i.e., to allow more people than was originally intended, (which is outlined in the agreement) to live in the property. If a tenant does, then the landlord can take action to evict.

Different types of tenancy agreement

The protected tenancy - the meaning of the term

As a basic guide, if a person is a private tenant and signed their current agreement with a landlord before 15th January 1989 then they will, in most cases, be a protected tenant with all the rights relating to protection of tenure, which are considerable. Protection is provided under the 1977 Rent Act. In practice, there are not many protected tenancies left and the tenant will usually be signing an assured shorthold tenancy..

The assured shorthold tenancy - what it means

If the tenant entered into an agreement with a landlord after 15th January 1989 then they will, in most cases, be an assured tenant. We will discuss assured tenancies in more depth in the next chapter In brief, there are various types of assured tenancy. The assured shorthold is usually a fixed term version of the assured tenancy and enables the landlord to recover their property after six months and to vary the rent after this time.

At this point it is important to understand that the main difference between the two types of tenancy, protected and assured, is that the tenant has less rights as a tenant under the assured tenancy. For example, they will not be entitled, as is a protected tenant, to a fair rent set by a Rent Officer.

Other types of agreement

In addition to the above tenancy agreements, there are other types of agreement sometimes used in privately rented property. One of these is the company let, as we discussed in the last chapter, and another is the license agreement. The person signing such an agreement is called a licensee.

Licenses will only apply in special circumstances where the licensee cannot be given sole occupation of his home and therefore can only stay for a short period with minimum rights.

Squatting

Under section 144 of the Legal Aid, Sentencing and Punishment of Offenders Act, which came into force on the first day of September 2012, squatting in residential buildings (like a house or flat) is illegal. It can lead to 6 months in prison, a £5,000 fine, or both. Squatting is when someone knowingly enters a residential building as a trespasser and lives there, or intends to live there.

A tenant who enters a property with the permission of the landlord, but who falls behind with rent payments, is **not** a squatter. Although squatting a non-residential building or land isn't in itself a crime, trespassers on non-residential property may be committing other crimes.

It's normally a crime for a person to enter private property without permission and refuse to leave when the owner asks. In certain circumstances, it may also be a crime if someone doesn't leave land when they've been directed to do so by the police or council, or if they don't comply with a repossession order.

Squatting in non-residential properties

A non-residential property is any building or land that isn't designed to be lived in.

Simply being on another person's non-residential property without their permission is not usually a crime. But if squatters commit other crimes when entering or staying in a property, the police can take action against them.

These crimes could include:

- causing damage when entering the property
- causing damage while in the property
- not leaving when they're told to by a court
- stealing from the property
- using utilities like electricity or gas without permission
- fly-tipping
- not complying with a noise abatement notice

Getting your non-residential property back
If a person owns the property that has been squatted, he or she can use an interim possession order (IPO) to get their property back quickly.

Court action
If the right procedure is followed, they can usually get one issued by the courts within a few days.

To get final possession of the property, they must also make an application for possession when they apply for the IPO.

Use form N130 to apply for an interim possession order and for possession.

Exceptions
You can't use an IPO if:

- you're also making a claim for damages caused by the squatters - instead you can make an ordinary claim for possession
- more than 28 days have passed since you found out about the squatters
- you're trying to evict former tenants, sub-tenants or licensees Once squatters are served with an IPO, they must leave the property within 24 hours. If they don't, they're committing a crime and could serve up to 6 months in prison.

It's also a crime for them to return to the property within 12 months.

Squatters taking ownership of a property

It's difficult and very rare for squatters to take ownership of a property. To do this, they would have to stay in a property without the owner's permission for at least 10 years.

5

ASSURED TENANTS

The assured tenant

As we have seen, with the exception of local authority tenancies, all tenancies, (with the main exceptions detailed), are known as assured tenancies. An assured shorthold, which is the most common form of tenancy used by the landlord nowadays, is one type of assured tenancy, and is for a fixed term of six months minimum and can be brought to an end with two months notice by serving a section 21 (of the Housing Act 1988) notice.

It is important to note that all tenancies signed after February 1997 are assured shorthold agreements unless otherwise stated.

Assured tenancies are governed by the 1988 Housing Act, as amended by the 1996 Housing Act. It is to these Acts, or outlines of the Acts that the tenant must refer when intending to sign a tenancy for a residential property.

For a tenancy to be assured, three conditions must be fulfilled:

1. The premises must be a dwelling house. This basically means any premises which can be lived in. Business premises will normally fall outside this interpretation.
2. There must exist a particular relationship between landlord and tenant. In other words there must exist a tenancy agreement. For example, a license to occupy, as in the case of students, or accommodation occupied as a result of work, cannot be seen as a tenancy. Following on from this, the accommodation must be let as a single unit. The tenant, who must be an individual, must normally be able to sleep, cook and eat in the accommodation. Sharing of bathroom facilities will not

prevent a tenancy being an assured tenancy but shared cooking or other facilities, such as a living room, will.

3. The third requirement for an assured tenancy is that the tenant must occupy the dwelling as his or her only or principal home. In situations involving joint tenants at least one of them must occupy.

Tenancies that are not assured

A tenancy agreement will not be assured if one of the following conditions applies:

-The tenancy or the contract was entered into before 15th January 1989;

-If no rent is payable or if only a low rent amounting to less than two thirds of the present ratable value of the property is payable;

-If the premises are let for business purposes or for mixed residential and business purposes;

-If part of the dwelling house is licensed for the sale of liquor for consumption on the premises. This does not include the publican who lets out a flat;

-If the dwelling house is let with more than two acres of agricultural land;

-If the dwelling house is part of an agricultural holding and is occupied in relation to carrying out work on the holding;

-If the premises are let by a specified institution to students, i.e., halls of residence;

-If the premises are let for the purpose of a holiday;

-Where there is a resident landlord, e.g., in the case where the landlord has let one of his rooms but continues to live in the house;

-If the landlord is the Crown (the monarchy) or a government department. Certain lettings by the Crown are capable of being assured, such as some lettings by the Crown Estate Commissioners;

-If the landlord is a local authority, a fully mutual housing association (this is where you have to be a shareholder to be a tenant) a newly created Housing Action Trust or any similar body listed in the 1988 Housing Act.

-If the letting is transitional such as a tenancy continuing in its original form until phased out, such as:

-A protected tenancy under the 1977 Rent Act;

-Secure tenancy granted before 1st January 1989, e.g., from a local authority or housing association. These tenancies are governed by the 1985 Housing Act).

The Assured Shorthold tenancy

The assured shorthold tenancy as we have seen, is the most common form of tenancy used in the private sector. The main principle of the assured shorthold tenancy is that it is issued for a period of six months minimum and can be brought to an end by the landlord serving two-months notice on the tenant. (A S21 notice cannot be served if a landlord has not served the required deposit prescribed terms and conditions, if taking a deposit). At the end of the six-month period the tenant, if given two months prior notice, must leave.

Any property let on an assured tenancy can be let on an assured shorthold, providing the following three conditions are met:

- The tenancy must be for a fixed term of not less than six months.
- The agreement cannot contain powers which enable the landlord to end the tenancy before six months. This does not include the right of the landlord to enforce the grounds for possession, which will be approximately the same as those for the assured tenancy (see below).
- A notice requiring possession at the end of the term is usually served two months before that date.
- A notice must be served before any rent increase giving one months clear notice and providing details of the rent increase.

If the landlord wishes to get possession of his/her property, in this case before the expiry of the contractual term, the landlord has to gain a court order. A notice of seeking possession must be served, giving fourteen days notice and following similar grounds of possession as an assured tenancy. *The landlord cannot simply tell a tenant to leave before the end of the agreed term.*

If the tenancy runs on after the end of the fixed term then the landlord can regain possession by giving the required two months notice, as mentioned above.

At the end of the term for which the assured shorthold tenancy has been granted, the landlord has an automatic right to possession.

An assured shorthold tenancy will become periodic (will run from week to week) when the initial term of six months has elapsed and the landlord has not brought the tenancy to an end. A periodic tenancy is brought to an end with two months notice.

Assured shorthold tenants can be evicted only on certain grounds, some discretionary, some mandatory (see below).

In order for the landlord of an assured shorthold tenant to regain possession of the property, a notice of seeking possession (of property) must be served, giving fourteen days notice of expiry and stating the ground for possession. A copy of this notice is shown in Appendix 2. This notice is similar to a notice to quit, discussed in the previous chapter.

Following the fourteen days a court order must be obtained. Although gaining a court order is not complicated, a solicitor will usually be used. Court costs can be awarded against the tenant.

Security of tenure: The ways in which a tenant can lose their home as an assured shorthold tenant

There are a number of circumstances called grounds (mandatory and discretionary) whereby a landlord can start a court action to evict a tenant.

The following are the *mandatory* grounds (where the judge must give the landlord possession) and *discretionary* grounds (where the judge does not have to give the landlord possession) on which a court can order possession if the home is subject to an assured tenancy.

The mandatory grounds for possession of a property let on an assured (shorthold) tenancy

There are eight mandatory grounds for possession, which, if proved, leave the court with no choice but to make an order for possession. It is very important that you understand these.

Ground One is used where the landlord has served a notice, no later than at the beginning of the tenancy, warning the tenant that this ground may be used against him/her.

This ground is used where the landlord wishes to recover the property as his or her principal (first and only) home or the spouse's (wife's or husbands) principal home. ***The ground is not available to a person who bought the premises for gain (profit) whilst they were occupied.***

Ground Two is available where the property is subject to a mortgage and if the landlord does not pay the mortgage, could lose the home.

Grounds Three and Four relate to holiday lettings.

Ground Five is a special one, applicable to ministers of religion.

Ground Six relates to the demolition or reconstruction of the property.

Ground Seven applies if a tenant dies and in his will leaves the tenancy to someone else: but the landlord must start proceedings against the new tenant within a year of the death if he wants to evict the new tenant.

Ground Eight concerns rent arrears. This ground applies if, both at the date of the serving of the notice seeking possession and at the date of the hearing of the action, the rent is at least 8 weeks in arrears or two months in arrears. This is the main ground used by landlords when rent is not being paid.

The discretionary grounds for possession of a property, which is let on an assured tenancy

As we have seen, the discretionary grounds for possession are those in relation to which the court has some powers over whether or not the landlord can evict. In other words, the final decision is left to the judge. Often the judge will prefer to grant a suspended order first, unless the circumstances are dramatic.

Ground Nine applies when suitable alternative accommodation is available or will be when the possession order takes effect. As we have seen, if the landlord wishes to obtain possession of his or her property in order to use it for other purposes then suitable alternative accommodation has to be provided.

Ground Ten deals with rent arrears as does *ground eleven.* These grounds are distinct from the mandatory grounds, as there does not have to be a fixed arrear in terms of time scale, e.g., 8 weeks. The judge, therefore, has some choice as to whether or not to evict. In practice, this ground will not be relevant to managers of assured shorthold tenancies.

Ground Twelve concerns any broken obligation of the tenancy. As we have seen with the protected tenancy, there are a number of conditions of the tenancy agreement, such as the requirement not to racially or sexually harass a neighbor. Ground Twelve will be used if these conditions are broken.

Ground Thirteen deals with the deterioration of the dwelling as a result of a tenant's neglect. This is connected with the structure of the property and is the same as for a protected tenancy. It puts the responsibility on the tenant to look after the premises.

Ground Fourteen concerns nuisance, annoyance and illegal or immoral use. This is where a tenant or anyone connected with the tenant has caused a nuisance to neighbors.

Ground 14A this ground deals with domestic violence.

Ground 15 concerns the condition of the furniture and tenants neglect. As Ground thirteen puts some responsibility on the tenant to look after the structure of the building so Ground Fifteen makes the tenant responsible for the furniture and fittings.

Ground 16 covers former employees. The premises were let to a former tenant by a landlord seeking possession and the tenant has ceased to be in that employment.

Ground 17 is where a person or that persons agents makes a false or reckless statement and this has caused the landlord to grant the tenancy under false pretences.

The description of the grounds above is intended as a guide only. For a fuller description please refer to the 1988 Housing Act, section 7, Schedule two,) as amended by the 1996 Housing Act) which is available at reference libraries.

Fast track possession

In November 1993, following changes to the County Court Rules, a facility was introduced which enabled landlords of tenants with assured shorthold tenancies to apply for possession of their property without the usual time delay involved in waiting for a court date and attendance at court. This is known as "fast track possession" It cannot be used for rent arrears or other grounds. It is used to gain possession of a property when the fixed term of six months or more has come to an end and the tenant will not move.

Payment of rent

If the landlord wishes to raise rent, at least one month's minimum notice must be given. The rent cannot be raised more than once for the same tenant in one year. Tenants have the right to challenge a rent increase if they think it is unfair by referring the rent to a Rent Assessment

Committee. The committee will prevent the landlord from raising the rent above the ordinary market rent for that type of property. We will be discussing rent and rent control further on in this book.

6

JOINT TENANCIES

Joint tenancies: the position of two or more people who have a tenancy agreement for one property

Although it is the normal state of affairs for a tenancy agreement to be granted to one person, this is not always the case.

A tenancy can also be granted to two or more people and is then known as a *joint tenancy*. The position of joint tenants is exactly the same as that of single tenants. In other words, there is still one tenancy even though it is shared.

Each tenant is responsible for paying the rent and observing the terms and conditions of the tenancy agreement. No one joint tenant can prevent another joint tenant's access to the premises.

If one of the joint tenants dies then his or her interest will automatically pass to the remaining joint tenants. A joint tenant cannot dispose of his or her interest in a will.

If one joint tenant, however, serves a notice to quit (notice to leave the property) on another joint tenant(s) then the tenancy will come to an end and the landlord can apply to court for a possession order, if the remaining tenant does not leave.

The position of a wife or husband in relation to joint tenancies is rather more complex because the married person has more rights when it comes to the home than the single person.

Remember: the position of a tenant who has signed a joint tenancy agreement is exactly the same as that of the single tenant. If one person leaves, the other(s) have the responsibilities of the tenancy. If one person leaves without paying his share of the rent then the other tenants will have to pay instead.

7

RENT AND OTHER CHARGES

The payment of rent and other financial matters

If a tenancy is protected under the Rent Act 1977, as described earlier there is the right to apply to the Rent Officer for the setting of a fair rent for the property.

The assured tenant

The assured tenant has far fewer rights in relation to rent control than the protected tenant.

The Housing Act 1988 allows a landlord to charge whatever he likes. There is no right to a fair or reasonable rent with an assured tenancy. If the tenancy is assured then there will usually be a formula in the tenancy which will provide guidance for rent increases. If not then the landlord can set what rent he or she likes within reason. If the amount is unreasonable then the tenant can refer the matter to the rent assessment committee. The rent can sometimes be negotiated at the outset of the tenancy. This rent has to be paid as long as the contractual term of the tenancy lasts. Once the contractual term has expired, the landlord is entitled to continue to charge the same rent.

On expiry of an assured shorthold the landlord is free to grant a new tenancy and set the rent to a level that is compatible with the market.

Rent control for assured shorthold tenants

We have seen that the assured shorthold tenancy is for a minimum period of six months. Like the assured tenant, the assured shorthold tenant has no right to request that a fair rent should be set. The rent is a market rent.

As with an assured tenancy, the assured shorthold tenant has the right to appeal to a Rent Assessment Committee in the case of what he/she considers an unreasonable rent. This may be done during the contractual term of the tenancy. The Committee will consider whether the rent is significantly higher than is usual for a similar property.

If the Committee assesses a different rent from that set by the landlord, they may set a date when the increase will take effect. The rent cannot be backdated to before the date of the application. Once a decision has been reached by the Committee, the landlord cannot increase the rent for at least twelve months, or on termination of the tenancy. Details of the local Rent Assessment Committee can be obtained from the Rent Officer Service at your local authority.

Housing Benefit

Housing benefit is a benefit for people on low income to help them pay their rent. You may be able to get housing benefit if you are on other benefits or work part time or full time on a low income.

To get housing benefit in the first place you must pay rent. It doesn't matter who the landlord is, whether private or public sector. You can also claim housing benefit if you rent a room in a hostel or are a boarder. You can claim it if you share a house or flat as point or sub-tenants. You cannot get housing benefit if you rent your home from the Crown, or you are 16 or 17 or have been in care.

Only one member of a couple who live together can claim housing benefit. You must also live in the accommodation for which you are claiming benefit. Since April 2013, different rules apply to public sector tenants, who will be affected by the 'bedroom tax'. Essentially, housing benefit is reduced depending on the size of the property and the extent of under occupation. the rules below relate to private tenants.

UK Resident

You must be living in the UK to claim housing benefit. If you are from overseas or have recently arrived in the UK you may have difficulty claiming housing benefit.

Income and capital

To get housing benefit you must have income and capital below a certain level. Capital means savings, land, property or anything else that could provide you with an income. If you have more than £16,000 in capital you will not get housing benefit, unless you are getting the guarantee part of pension credit. If you have capital of over £6,000 you will be assumed to have some income from that capital.

If you are getting income support or income based jobseekers allowance, you will automatically be within the income and capital limits for housing benefits. If you are in pension credit and get the guarantee credit (whether on its own or with the savings credit) you will also automatically get the maximum housing benefit amount.

How much benefit can you get?

How much benefit you will get depends on how much rent you pay, what income you have and where you live. The rules for HB allowance are changing which are outlined below. If you pay rent to a private landlord, the rent your housing benefit will cover will normally be restricted to an amount set by the rent officer. When you make a new claim for housing benefit your local authority will normally calculate how much rent your housing benefit can cover suing the Local Authority Housing Allowance Rules. In many cases, however, the amount of HB that you are entitled to will not cover the full amount and you will have to make up the shortfall. There are different rules concerning applications for HB before and after 7th April 2008 and these rules can be obtained from the local authority.

There will be a limit on payments so that the Local Housing Allowance does not exceed:

- £250 per week for a one bedroom property (including shared accommodation)
- £290 a week for a two bedroom property
- £340 a week for a three bedroom property
- £400 a week for a four bedroom property

The maximum rate of HB will be limited to a four-bedroom property. There will be help for disabled people towards the cost of an extra bedroom if they need an overnight carer. Housing benefit is included in the overall cap on benefits that single people and couples can receive.

Shared room rate

This applies to single people under the age of 35 living in accommodation that they rent from a private landlord. Housing benefit is restricted to the average that a single person would pay for a shared house in an area. Previously, the rule applied to those under 25. There are exemptions: single 25-34 year olds who have lived in a homeless hostel for more than three months will still be entitled to a one bed flat, a single 25-34 year old ex-offender who is managed under Multi-Agency Public Protection Arrangements (MAPPA) is exempt and will not be expected to live in shared accommodation. In addition, a person under 22 who has been in care and receives Disability Living Allowance at the medium or higher rate for a severe disability will be exempt.

The above outline of housing benefit is very brief. The local authority in your area will be able to furnish you with full details.

Council tax and the tenant

Council tax is based on properties, or dwellings, and not individual people.

This means that there is one bill for each individual dwelling, rather than separate bills for each person. The number and type of people who live in the dwelling may affect the size of the final bill. A discount of 25% is given for people who live alone. Each property is placed in a valuation band with different properties paying more or less depending on their individual value. Tenants who feel that their home has been placed in the wrong valuation band can appeal to their local authority council tax department.

Who has to pay the council tax?

In most cases the tenant occupying the dwelling will have to pay the council tax. However, a landlord will be responsible for paying the council tax where there are several households living in one dwelling. This will usually be hostels, bedsits and other non-self contained flats where people share things such as cooking and washing facilities. The council tax on this type of property remains the responsibility of the landlord even if all but one of the tenants move out. Although the landlord has the responsibility for paying the council tax, he/she will normally try to pass on the increased cost through rents. However, as we have seen, there is a set procedure for a landlord to follow if he/she wishes to increase rent.

Council tax benefits available for those on low income

Tenants on very low income, except for students, will usually be able to claim a council tax reduction. This used to cover up to 100% of the council tax. However, with the widespread changes to benefits in 2013, council tax benefit has now been abolished (after April 2013) and each local authority will be responsible for payment of council tax reduction to individual tenants. Invariably, this will not be 100% so tenants will now be left with a shortfall that they will have to meet.

Tenants with disabilities may be entitled to further discounts. Tenants who are not responsible for individual council tax, but pay it through their rent, can claim housing benefit to cover the increase.

The rules covering council tax liability can be obtained from a Citizens Advice Bureau or from your local authority council tax department.

Service charges

A service charge covers provision of services other than those covered by the rent. A rental payment will normally cover maintenance charges, loan charges if any, and also profit. Other services, such as cleaning and gardening, will be covered by a separate charge, known as a service charge. A *registered* rent reflects the cost of any services provided by the landlord. An assured rent set by a landlord will normally include services, which must be outlined in the agreement.

The fact that the charges are variable must be written into a tenancy agreement and the landlord has a legal duty to provide the tenant with annual budgets and accounts and has to consult when he or she wishes to spend over a certain amount of money, currently £250 per dwelling or £100 for contracts such as cleaning and lift maintenance if they are for more than 12 months.

The form of consultation, which must take place, is that of writing to all those affected and informing them of:

-The landlord's intention to carry out work;

-Why these works are seen to be necessary;

This first notice is for 30 days after which another notice must be sent containing:

-The estimated cost of the works;
-At least two estimates or inviting residents to see two estimates.

A period of twenty-eight days must be allowed before work is carried out. This gives time for any feedback from tenants.

The landlord can incur reasonable expense, without consultation, if the work is deemed to be necessary, i.e. emergency works.

If a service charge is variable then a landlord has certain legal obligations, which are clearly laid out in the 1985 and 1987 Landlord and Tenant Acts as amended by the 2002 Commonhold and Leasehold Reform Act.

8

THE RIGHT TO QUIET ENJOYMENT OF A HOME

Earlier, we saw that when a tenancy agreement is signed, the landlord is contracting to give quiet enjoyment of the tenant's home. This means that they have the right to live peacefully in the home without harassment.

The landlord is obliged not to do anything that will disturb the right to the quiet enjoyment of the home. The most serious breach of this right would be for the landlord to wrongfully evict a tenant.

Eviction: what can be done against unlawful harassment and eviction
It is a criminal offence for a landlord unlawfully to evict a residential occupier (whether or not a tenant!). The occupier has protection under the Protection from Eviction Act 1977 section 1(2).

If the tenant or occupier is unlawfully evicted his/her first course should be to seek an injunction compelling the landlord to readmit him/her to the premises. It is an unfortunate fact but many landlords will attempt to evict tenants forcefully. In doing so they break the law.

However, the landlord may, on termination of the tenancy recover possession without a court order if the agreement was entered into after 15th January 1989 and it falls into one of the following six situations:

- The occupier shares any accommodation with the landlord and the landlord occupies the premises as his or her only or principal home.

- The occupier shares any of the accommodation with a member of the landlords family, that person occupies the premises as their only or principal home, and the landlord occupies as his or her only or principal home premises in the same building.

- The tenancy or license was granted temporarily to an occupier who entered the premises as a trespasser.
- The tenancy or license gives the right to occupy for the purposes of a holiday.
- The tenancy or license is rent-free.
- The license relates to occupation of a hostel.

There is also a section in the 1977 Protection from Eviction Act which provides a defense for otherwise unlawful eviction and that is that the landlord may repossess if it is thought that the tenant no longer lives on the premises. It is important to note that, in order for such action to be seen as a crime under the 1977 Protection from Eviction Act, the intention of the landlord to evict must be proved. However, there is another offence, namely harassment, which also needs to be proved. Even if the landlord is not guilty of permanently depriving a tenant of their home he/she could be guilty of harassment. Such actions as cutting off services, deliberately allowing the premises to fall into a state of disrepair, or even forcing unwanted sexual attentions, all constitute harassment and a breach of the right to *quiet enjoyment.*

The 1977 Protection from Eviction Act also prohibits the use of violence to gain entry to premises. Even in situations where the landlord has the right to gain entry without a court order it is an offence to use violence.

If entry to the premises is opposed then the landlord should gain a court order.

What can be done against unlawful evictions?

There are two main remedies for unlawful eviction: damages and, as stated above, an injunction. An injunction is an order from the court requiring a person to do, or not to do something. In the case of eviction the court can grant an injunction requiring the landlord to allow a tenant back into occupation of the premises. In the case of harassment an order can be made preventing the landlord from harassing the tenant.

Failure to comply with an injunction is contempt of court and can result in a fine or imprisonment.

Damages

In some cases the tenant can press for *financial compensation* following unlawful eviction. Financial compensation may have to be paid in cases where financial loss has occurred or in cases where personal hardship alone has occurred.

The tenant can also press for *special damages,* which means that the tenant may recover the definable out-of-pocket expenses. These could be expenses arising as a result of having to stay in a hotel because of the eviction. Receipts must be kept in that case. There are also *general damages,* which can be awarded in compensation for stress, suffering and inconvenience.

A tenant may also seek *exemplary damages* where it can be proved that the landlord has disregarded the law deliberately with the intention of making a profit out of the displacement of the tenant.

9

REPAIRS-LANDLORDS/TENANTS OBLIGATIONS

Repairs and improvements generally: The landlord and tenants obligations

Repairs are essential works to keep the property in good order. Improvements and alterations to the property, e.g. the installation of a shower.

As we have seen, most tenancies are periodic, i.e. week-to-week or month-to-month. If a tenancy falls into this category, or is a fixed-term tenancy for less than seven years, and began after October 1961, then a landlord is legally responsible for most major repairs to the flat or house.

If a tenancy began after 15th January 1989 then, in addition to the above responsibility, the landlord is also responsible for repairs to common parts and service fittings.

The area of law dealing with the landlord and tenants repairing obligations is the 1985 Landlord and Tenant Act, section 11.

This section of the Act is known as a covenant and cannot be excluded by informal agreement between landlord and tenant. In other words the landlord is legally responsible whether he or she likes it or not. Parties to a tenancy, however, may make an application to a court mutually to vary or exclude this section.

Example of repairs a landlord is responsible for:

- Leaking roofs and guttering.

- Rotting windows.
- Rising damp.
- Damp walls.
- Faulty electrical wiring.
- Dangerous ceilings and staircases.
- Faulty gas and water pipes.
- Broken water heaters and boilers.
- Broken lavatories, sinks or baths.

In shared housing the landlord must see that shared halls, stairways, kitchens and bathrooms are maintained and kept clean and lit.

Normally, tenants are responsible only for minor repairs, e.g., broken door handles, cupboard doors, etc. Tenants will also be responsible for decorations unless they have been damaged as a result of the landlord's failure to do repair.

A landlord will be responsible for repairs only if the repair has been reported. It is therefore important to report repairs in writing and keep a copy. If the repair is not carried out then action can be taken. Damages can also be claimed.

Compensation can be claimed, with the appropriate amount being the reduction in the value of the premises to the tenant caused by the landlord's failure to repair. If the tenant carries out the repairs then the amount expended will represent the decrease in value.

The tenant does not have the right to withhold rent because of a breach of repairing covenant by the landlord. However, depending on the repair, the landlord will not have a very strong case in court if rent is withheld.

Reporting repairs to landlords

The tenant has to tell the landlord or the person collecting the rent straight away when a repair needs doing. It is advisable that it is in writing, listing the repairs that need to be done.

Once a tenant has reported a repair the landlord must do it within a reasonable period of time. What is reasonable will depend on the nature of the repair. If certain emergency work needs to be done by the council, such as leaking guttering or drains a notice can be served ordering the landlord to do the work within a short time. In exceptional cases if a home cannot be made habitable at reasonable cost the council may declare that the house must no longer be used, in which case the council has a legal duty to re-house a tenant.

If after the council has served notice the landlord still does not do the work, the council can send in its own builder or, in some cases take the landlord to court. A tenant must allow a landlord access to do repairs. The landlord has to give twenty-four hours notice of wishing to gain access.

The tenants rights whilst repairs are being carried out

The landlord must ensure that the repairs are done in an orderly and efficient way with minimum inconvenience to the tenant. If the works are disruptive or if property or decorations are damaged the tenant can apply to the court for compensation or, if necessary, for an order to make the landlord behave reasonably.

If the landlord genuinely needs the house empty to do the work he/she can ask the tenant to vacate it and can if necessary get a court order against the tenant.

A written agreement should be drawn up making it clear that the tenant can move back in when the repairs are completed and stating what the arrangements for fuel charges and rent are.

If a person is an assured tenant the landlord could get a court order to make that person give up the home permanently if there is work to be done with him/her in occupation.

Can the landlord put the rent up after doing repairs?

If there is a service charge for maintenance, the landlord may be able to pass on the cost of the work(s).

Tenants rights to make improvements to a property

Unlike carrying out repairs the tenant will not normally have the right to insist that the landlord make actual alterations to the home. However, a tenant needs the following amenities and the law states that you should have:

- Bath or shower.
- Wash hand basin.
- Hot and cold water at each bath, basin or shower.
- An indoor toilet.

If these amenities do not exist then the tenant can contact the council's Environmental Health Officer. An improvement notice can be served on the landlord ordering him to put the amenity in.

Disabled tenants

If a tenant is disabled he/she may need special items of equipment in the accommodation. The local authority may help in providing and, occasionally, paying for these. The tenant will need to obtain the permission of the landlord. If you require more information then contact the social services department locally.

The Equality Act 2010

The Equality Act 2010 has introduced a new duty on landlords (from October 2010) to consent to changes in common parts of residential or mixed-use buildings in England, Wales and Scotland. This means that if a disabled tenant or occupier who uses or intends to use premises in a building as his or her main home requests physical changes to common parts to reduce or avoid a disadvantage suffered in comparison with non-disabled people, the landlord must within a reasonable time consult all other likely to be affected by the changes and, having considered the views of those consulted, take whatever steps are reasonable to avoid the disadvantage. If changes to the common parts are considered reasonable the landlord must first enter into a written agreement that the disabled person organizes and pays for the work and for restoration of the common parts when the disabled person leaves the property.

The agreement will bind the landlord's successors but not the disabled person's successors. So the landlord may wish to insist that the works are reinstated before the disabled person leaves.

Shared housing. The position of tenants in shared houses (Houses in Multiple Occupation)

A major change to improve standards of shared housing was introduced in 2006. The parts of the Housing Act 2004 relating to the licensing of HMO's (Houses in Multiple Occupation) and the new Health and Safety Rating System for assessing property conditions came into effect on 6rh April 2006.

The Act requires landlords of many HMO's to apply for licences. The HMO's that need to be licensed are those with:

- Three or more storeys, which are
- Occupied by five or more people forming two or more households (i.e. people not related, living together as a couple etc) and
- Which have an element of shared facilities (eg kitchen, bathroom etc)

As far as licensing is concerned, attics and basements are included as storeys if they are used as living accommodation. Previously, HMO's were only defined as houses converted into flats or bedsits, but the new Act widens this definition and many more types of shared houses are now included. A local authority will have a list of designated properties will have a list of those properties which are designated HMO's and they will need to be licensed.

Usually, landlords will need to apply to a local authority private sector unit for licences. It has been illegal for landlords to manage designated properties without a licence since July 2006.

Landlords will have to complete an application form and pay a fee, the local authority will then assess whether the property is suitable for the number of people the landlord wants to rent it to. In most case, the local authority, their agents, will visit a property to assess facilities and also fire precautions. A decision will then be taken to grant a license.

There is a fee for registration, councils set the fee and the ones shown below are indicative of a southern local authority:

- Shared houses-five sharers landlords first house £640
- Subsequent house £590
- Plus £10 each additional occupier over five

Hostels
- 10 occupiers £690
- 20 occupiers £790
- 50 occupiers £1100
- 75 occupiers £1340

In summary, The landlord of a HMO has certain duties under the regulations to his tenants:

Duty to provide information
The manager (this means that whoever is charged with the management of the building) must ensure that:
- His name, address and telephone number are available to each household in the HMO

- These details are also clearly displayed in a prominent position in the HMO.

The manager should maintain a log book to record all events at the property such as:

- Testing of fire alarms
- Testing of fire fighting equipment
- Gas safety certificate
- Electrical report
- Inspection and wants of repair

Duty to take safety measures

The manager must ensure that all means of escape from fire in the property are kept free from obstruction and in good order as should all fire alarms and equipment.

The manager should ensure that the structure is designed and maintained in a safe condition, and also take steps to protect occupiers from injury. In properties with four or more occupants, the Regulations provide that fire escape notices be clearly displayed.

Duty to maintain water supply drainage

The manager must ensure that the water supply and drainage system serving the property are maintained in a good working condition. More specifically, water fittings should be protected from frost and all water storage tanks should be provided with covers.

Duty to supply and maintain gas and electricity

The manager must supply the local housing authority within 7 days of receiving a written request a safety certificate. The manager must ensure that the fixed electrical installation is checked at least once every three years by a suitably qualified electrician and supply this to the LHA on written request.

In addition to the above, there is a duty to maintain common parts, fixtures, fittings and appliances. There is a duty to maintain living accommodation and to provide waste disposal facilities.

Powers of the local authority in relation to HMO's

It is essential to ensure that, if you have invested in a HMO that you manage it rigorously because local authorities have sweeping powers to fine landlords and to revoke licenses. A local authority can prosecute a landlord who does not obtain a license for a HMO.

Safety generally for all landlords-the regulations

The main product safety regulations relevant to the lettings industry are:

Gas safety
The Gas safety (Installation and use) Regulations 1998
The Gas Cooking Appliances (safety) Regulations 1989
Heating Appliances(Fireguard) (safety) Regulations 1991
Gas Appliances(Safety) Regulations 1995

All of the above are based on the fact that the supply of gas and the appliances in a dwelling are safe. A Gas Safety certificate is required to validate this.

Furniture Safety
Furniture and Furnishings (Fire) (Safety) Regulations 1988 and 1993 (as amended)

Landlords and lettings agents are included in these regulations. The regulations set high standards for fire resistance for domestic upholstered furniture and other products containing upholstery. The main provisions are:

- Upholstered articles (i.e. beds, sofas, armchairs etc) must have fire resistant filling material.
- Upholstered articles must have passed a match resistant test or, if of certain kinds (such as cotton or silk) be used with a fire resistant interliner.
- The combination of the cover fabric and the filling material must have passed a cigarette resistance test.

The landlord should inspect property for non-compliant items before letting and replace with compliant items.

Electrical Safety

Electrical Equipment (Safety) Regulations 1994

Plugs and Sockets etc. (Safety) Regulations 1994.

The Electrical Equipment Regulations came into force in January 1995. Both sets of regulations relate to the supply of electrical equipment designed with a working voltage of between 50 and 1000 volts a.c. (or between 75 and 1000 volts d.c.) the regulations cover all the mains voltage household electrical goods including cookers, kettles, toasters, electric blankets, washing machines, immersion heaters etc. The regulations do not apply to items attached to land. This is generally considered to exclude the fixed wiring and built in appliances (e.g. central heating systems) from the regulations.

The availability of grants
Disabled Facilities Grant

The only mandatory grant is the Disabled Facilities Grant, given to those in need, which has been assessed by an Occupational Therapist-the grant has a ceiling. Information of which can be obtained from the local authority. As the name suggests it is for those who are disabled and are n need of works which will make the property accessible and usable for disabled people.

Disabled Facilities Assistance

Disabled Facilities Assistance is in the form of interest free loans, repayable on disposal of the property. To qualify for DFA a person must be at least 18 years old and a freeholder or leaseholder with at least 10 years to expiry of lease and authority to do the work. The maximum amount of assistance is £25,000 or 50% of the equity existing at the time of application. There are a number of other conditions related to the actual works. Details can be obtained from the local authority.

Decent Homes Loans Assistance

This is available to homeowners to enable them to bring their property up to the national Decent Homes Standard. Homes meet Decent Homes standard if they meet a set of criteria which is laid down by the government, such as thermal insulation, overall state of repair etc. Details of the standards can be obtained from the local authority. There are a number of property related criteria and as the money offered is a loan then it will be means tested.

Common Parts Loan/ Common Parts Assistance

This help and assistance is available to owner occupiers (leaseholders) to assist them to meet their liabilities towards the cost of major refurbishment of the common parts of buildings containing their flats, where one or more of the key components of the common parts are old and require replacement or major repair, leading to one or more of the flats becoming 'non-decent' as defined in government guidance. Key components include external walls, roof structure and covering, chimneys etc. Common parts loans are administered by a third party and offered at a subsidised interest rate. They are repayable on disposal of the property.

The criteria for Common Part Loans can be obtained from the local authority.

Landlords Major Works Assistance

Local authorities will usually consider assistance to landlords who elect to bring empty properties back into use as accommodation for homeless people. This will involve leasing properties back to the council for a ten-year period. This scheme will depend on the policy of the local authority.

Minor work assistance

Grants are sometimes available to owner-occupiers and tenants for small-scale work for which they have the responsibility. The aim of such grants will be to ensure the person involved achieves the decent homes standard, improves energy efficiency, improves security or to carry out disabled adaptations as an alternative to DFG.

Details of these various grants and the criteria attached to them can be obtained from the local authority.

Energy Innovation Grants

These grants are subject to the availability of funding and are related to the policy of the local authority.

Sanitation health and hygiene

Local authorities have a duty to serve an owner with a notice requiring the provision of a WC when a property has insufficient sanitation, sanitation meaning toilet waste disposal. They will also serve notice if it is thought that the existing sanitation is inadequate and is harmful to health or is a nuisance. Local authorities have similar powers under various Public Health Acts to require owners to put right bad drains and sewers, also food storage facilities and vermin, plus the containing of disease.

The Environmental Health Department, if it considers the problem bad enough will serve a notice requiring the landlord to put the defect right. In certain cases the local authority can actually do the work and require the landlord to pay for it. This is called work in default.

10

WHAT SHOULD BE PROVIDED UNDER THE TENANCY

Furniture

A private landlords decision whether or not to furnish property will depend on the sort of tenant that he is aiming to find. The actual legal distinction between a furnished property and an unfurnished property has faded into insignificance.

If a landlord does let a property as furnished then the following would be the absolute minimum:

- Seating, such as sofa and armchair

- Cabinet or sideboard

- Kitchen tables and chairs

- Cooker and refrigerator

- Bedroom furniture

Even unfurnished lets, however, are expected to come complete with a basic standard of furniture, particularly carpets and kitchen goods. If the landlord does supply electrical equipment then he or she is able to disclaim any repairing responsibility for it, but this must be mentioned in the tenancy agreement.

Services

Usually, a landlord will only provide services to a tenant if the property is a flat situated in a block or is a house on a private estate. The services will include cyclical painting and maintenance, usually on a three to four year basis (flats) and gardening and cleaning plus repairs to the communal areas, plus communal electricity bills and water rates. These services should be outlined in the agreement and are administered within a strict framework of law, The 1985 Landlord and Tenant Act Section 18-30 as amended by the 1987 LTA and the 2002 Commonhold and Leasehold Reform Act. The landlord has rigid duties imposed within this Act, such as the need to gain estimates before commencing works and also to consult with residents where the cost exceeds £250 per flat or £100 for works based on an annual contract such as lift maintenance, gardening etc.. The landlord must give the tenant four weeks notice of intention to carry out works inviting feedback then a further four weeks notice with estimates.

Tenants have the right to see audited accounts and invoices relating to work. Service charges, as an extra payment over and above the rent are always contentious and it is an area that Landlords need to be aware of if they are to manage professionally.

Repairs
See chapter on repairing obligations

Insurance
Strictly speaking, there is no duty on either landlord or tenant to insure the property. However, it is highly advisable for the landlord to provide buildings insurance as he/she stands to lose a lot more in the event of fire or other disaster than the tenant. A landlord letting property for a first time would be well advised to consult his/ her insurance company before letting as there are different criteria to observe when a property is let and not to inform the company could invalidate the policy.

At the end of the tenancy
The tenancy agreement will normally spell out the obligations of the tenant at the end of the term. Essentially, the tenant will have an obligation to:

- have kept the interior clean and tidy and in a good state of repair and decoration
- have not caused any damage

- have replaced anything that they have broken
- replace or pay for the repair of anything that they have damaged
- pay for the laundering of the linen
- pay for any other laundering
- put anything that they have moved or removed back to how it was

Sometimes a tenancy agreement will make provision for the tenants paying for anything that is soiled at their own expense, although sensible wear and tear is allowed for.

The landlord will normally be able to recover any loss from the deposit that the tenant has given on entering the premises (see section on Deposit protection Scheme). However, sometimes, the tenants will withhold rent for the last month in order to recoup their deposit. It is up to the landlord to negotiate re-imbursement for any damage caused, but this should be within reason. There is a remedy, which can be pursued in the Small Claims court if the tenants refuse to pay but this is rarely successful.

11

GOING TO COURT TO REGAIN POSSESSION OF A HOME

There may come a time when the landlord needs to go to court to regain possession of his property. This will usually arise when the contract has been breached by the tenant, for non-payment of rent or for some other breach such as nuisance or harassment. As we have seen, a tenancy can be brought to an end in a court on one of the grounds for possession. However, as the tenancy will usually be an assured shorthold then it is necessary to consider whether you are in a position to be given two months notice, as opposed to going to court.

If the landlord decides, for whatever reasons, to go to court, then any move to regain a property for breach of agreement will commence in the county court in the area in which the property is. The first steps in ending the tenancy will necessitate the serving of a notice of seeking possession using one of the Grounds for Possession detailed earlier in the book. If the tenancy is protected then 28 days must be given, the notice must be in prescribed form and served on the tenant personally. See appendix for sample notice seeking possession.

If the tenancy is assured shorthold, which is usually always the case now, then 14 days notice of seeking possession can be used. In all cases the ground to be relied upon must be clearly outlined in the notice.

If the case is more complex, then this will entail a particulars of claim being prepared, usually by a solicitor, as opposed to a standard possession form. A fee is paid when sending the particulars to court.

The standard form which the landlord uses for routine rent arrears cases is called the N5 and there will be an accompanying Particulars of Claim. Both of these forms can be obtained from the court. When completed, the forms should be sent in duplicate to the county court and a copy retained for you.

The court will send a copy of the Particulars of claim and the summons to the tenant. They will send a form which gives the landlord a case number and court date to appear, known as the return date.

On the return date, if you are defending yourself you should arrive at court at least 15 minutes early. You can represent yourself in simple cases but are advised to use a solicitor for more contentious cases.

A number of orders are available. However, if the landlord has gone to court on the mandatory ground eight then if the fact is proved then he will get possession immediately. If not, then the judge can grant an order, suspended whilst the tenant finds time to pay.

Whatever the order, a bailiff's warrant will be needed to finally evict the tenant from the property. This can be obtained after the order is given by filling in the appropriate form and paying a fee to the bailiff office.

In a lot of cases, it is more expedient for a landlord to serve notice-requiring possession, if the tenancy has reached the end of the period, and then wait two months before the property is regained. This saves the cost and time of going to court particularly if the ground is one of nuisance or other, which will involve solicitors.

If a tenancy has reached the end of the contractual term and the landlord wish's to recover his property then a "fast track" procedure is available which entails gaining an order for possession and bailiff's order by post. This can be used in cases with the exception of rent arrears.

12

PUBLIC SECTOR TENANCIES

Renting from a social housing landlord
Who is a tenant of a social housing landlord

You are a tenant of a social housing landlord if you are a tenant of:

- a local authority. These are district councils and London borough councils; or
- a housing association; or
- a housing co-operative.

Local authority tenants

If you are a tenant of a local authority you are likely to be a secure tenant or an introductory tenant. In England, from 1 April 2012, local authorities can also grant flexible tenancies.

Housing association and housing co-operative tenants
Tenancy began before 15 January 1989

If you are a housing association or housing co-operative tenant and your tenancy began before 15 January 1989, you will be a secure tenant. For details about the rights a secure tenant has, see below.

Tenancy began on or after 15 January 1989

If you are a housing association or housing co-operative tenant and your tenancy began on or after 15 January 1989, you are likely to be an assured tenant. Some association tenants may be starter tenants for the first 12 to 18 months. A starter tenancy is a type of assured shorthold tenancy.

In England, from 1 April 2012, housing associations can use assured shorthold tenancies for tenancies other than starter tenancies.

Rights of secure tenants

As a secure tenant you have the right to stay in the accommodation unless your landlord can convince the court that there are special reasons to evict you, for example, you have rent arrears, damaged property or broken some other term of the agreement. As well as the right to stay in your home as long as you keep to the terms of the tenancy, you will also have other rights by law: These include the right:

- to have certain repairs carried out by your landlord
- to carry out certain repairs and to do improvements yourself - see under heading Repairs and improvements
- to sublet part of your home with your landlord's permission
- to take in lodgers without your landlord's permission
- to exchange your home with certain other social housing tenants
- if you are a local authority tenant, the right to vote to transfer to another landlord
- to be kept informed about things relating to your tenancy
- to buy your home.
- if you are a housing association tenant whose tenancy started before 15 January 1989, the right to a 'fair rent' - see under heading Fixing and increasing the rent
- for your spouse, civil partner, other partner or in some cases a resident member of your family, to take over the tenancy on your death (the right of 'succession')
- to assign (pass on) the tenancy to a person who has the right of 'succession' to the tenancy. This is sometimes difficult to enforce
- if you are a local authority tenant, to take over the management of the estate with other tenants by setting up a Tenant Management Organisation
- not to be discriminated against because of your disability, gender reassignment, pregnancy and maternity, race, religion or belief, sex or sexual orientation.

You will usually have a written tenancy agreement which may give you more rights than those set out above.

Complaints about secure tenancies

Each social housing landlord must have a clear policy and procedure on dealing with complaints. You should have the opportunity to complain in a range of ways. If after using your landlord's complaints procedure you are still dissatisfied, you can complain to an Ombudsman about certain problems. In England, if you are a local authority tenant this will be the Local Government Ombudsman, and if you are a housing association tenant it will be the Housing Ombudsman. If you have suffered discrimination, you can complain about this to the Ombudsman. In Wales, you can complain to the Public Services Ombudsman for Wales.

Rights of assured tenants

As an assured tenant you have the right to stay in your accommodation unless your landlord can convince the court there are reasons to evict you, for example, that there are rent arrears, damage to the property, or that another of the terms of the agreement has been broken.

As an assured tenant you can enforce your rights, for example, to get repairs done, without worrying about getting evicted. As well as the right to stay in your home as long as you keep to the terms of the tenancy you will also have other rights by law including:-

- the right to have the accommodation kept in a reasonable state of repair
- the right to carry out minor repairs yourself and to receive payment for these from your landlord - see under heading Repairs and improvements
- the right for your spouse, civil partner or other partner to take over the tenancy on your death (the right of 'succession')
- the right not to be treated unfairly by your landlord because of your disability, gender reassignment, pregnancy and maternity, race, religion or belief, sex or sexuality.

You will usually have a written tenancy agreement which may give you more rights than those set out above.

Complaints about assured tenancies

Each housing association must have a clear policy and procedure on dealing with complaints. You should have the opportunity to complain in a range of ways. If after using your landlord's complaints procedure you are still dissatisfied, you can complain in England, to the Housing Ombudsman, or in Wales, to the Public Services Ombudsman for Wales.

Starter tenancies and assured shorthold tenancies

A starter tenancy is the name often used by housing associations to describe an assured shorthold tenancy. Starter tenancies are probationary tenancies which allow a landlord to evict you more easily if you break the terms of your tenancy agreement.

A starter tenancy generally lasts for 12 months, although they can be extended to 18 months. As long as no action has been taken by the landlord to end the tenancy within the starter period, the starter tenant can then become an assured or longer-term assured shorthold tenant in England, or an assured tenant in Wales.

In England, housing associations can use assured shorthold tenancies for tenancies other than starter tenancies. They are likely to last for a fixed term of five years or more, but in some cases will last for two years. These tenancies may also be on 'affordable rent' terms.

In England, if you have an assured shorthold tenancy of a fixed term of two years or more with a housing association landlord, you will generally have similar rights to an assured tenant. However, if you have a fixed term tenancy, you only have the right to stay in your home for the length of the fixed term.

Complaints about starter and assured shorthold tenancies

Each housing association must have a clear policy and procedure on dealing with complaints. You should have the opportunity to complain in a range of ways. If after using your landlord's complaints procedure you are still dissatisfied, you can complain in England, to the Housing Ombudsman, or in Wales, to the Public Services Ombudsman for Wales.

Fixing and increasing the rent
Secure tenants
Local authority tenancies

Rents for local authority tenants are fixed according to the local authority's housing policy and the amount of money they get from central government. You cannot control the amount of rent payable, but may be able to claim housing benefit to help pay it.

Housing association and housing co-operative tenancies which began before 15 January 1989

If you are a housing association or housing co-operative tenant whose tenancy started before 15 January 1989 you are a secure tenant, but your rent is generally a 'fair rent' registered by the Rent Officer. The housing association or co-operative will usually have had the rent registered.

Once a rent has been registered, a new rent cannot usually be considered for the accommodation for two years. The rent can only be increased if:-

- you ask for a new fair rent assessment after two years
- your landlord asks for a new fair rent assessment after one year and nine months, although any new rent would not become effective until the end of two years.

An application for a rent increase can be made earlier, but only if the tenancy has changed drastically or if you and your landlord apply together. If you need help paying the rent you may be able to claim housing benefit.

Assured tenants
Housing association or housing co-operative tenancies which began on or after 15 January 1989

Many housing association tenants whose tenancy started on or after 15 January 1989 are assured tenants. If you are an assured tenant, your rent is the rent you agreed to pay your landlord at the beginning of the tenancy and should be covered in your tenancy agreement. The tenancy agreement should also state when and how the rent can be increased.

In England, most housing associations and housing co-operatives are registered with the Homes and Communities Agency and must follow standards and procedures set down by this regulatory body. They are sometimes known as social landlords. They set rents in accordance with government guidance and tenants have to be given clear information about how their rent and service charges are set and how they can be changed.

You may have the right to apply to a Rent Assessment Committee if you do not agree to a rent increase.

In Wales, housing associations must manage their housing to standards set by the Welsh Government. You must be informed in writing, and in advance about any changes in your rent. You should be given at least 28 days notice of any increase. You may have the right to apply to a Rent Assessment Committee if you do not agree to a rent increase.

If you are a housing association tenant in Wales, there is a leaflet explaining your rights called The Guarantee for Housing Association Residents. You can find this on the Welsh Government website at: www.new.wales.gov.uk.

If you want to apply to a Rent Assessment Committee you should consult an experienced adviser, for example, a Citizens Advice Bureau. If you need help paying the rent you may be able to claim housing benefit. You may also be entitled to other benefits if you are on a low income or you are unemployed.

To work out which other benefits you may be entitled to, you should consult an experienced adviser, for example, a Citizens Advice Bureau.

Affordable rent

Affordable rent is a type of social housing provided in England by social housing landlords.

The rent is called 'affordable' but it is a higher rent than would normally be charged for social housing. The landlord can charge up to 80% of what it would cost if you were renting the property privately. The extra money from affordable rent homes goes towards building more new social housing.

In most cases, tenancies on affordable rent terms are granted by housing associations. Where the landlord is a housing association, the type of tenancy granted is either an assured or an assured shorthold tenancy. In some cases, a local authority may grant a tenancy on affordable rent terms. Where it does, the tenancy type is either a secure or a flexible tenancy.

An affordable rent can be increased once a year. The maximum amount that an affordable rent can be increased by is Retail Price Index (RPI) + 0.5 %.

If you are on benefits or have a low income you may qualify for housing benefit to help pay some or all of the affordable rent.

Repairs and improvements

As a tenant you have the right to have your accommodation kept in a reasonable state of repair. You have also an obligation to look after the accommodation. The tenancy agreement may give more details of both your landlord's and your responsibilities in carrying out repairs and you should check this. We have discussed repairs earlier in the book.

Certain repairs will almost always be your landlord's responsibility, whether or not they are specifically mentioned in the tenancy agreement. These are:-

- the structure and exterior of the premises (such as walls, floors and window frames), and the drains, gutters and external pipes. If the property is a house, the essential means of access to it, such as steps from the street, are also included in 'structure and exterior'. It also includes garden paths and steps
- the water and gas pipes and electrical wiring (including, for example, taps and sockets)
- the basins, sinks, baths and toilets
- fixed heaters (for example, gas fires) and water heaters but not gas or electric cookers.

The Right to repair

Tenants of local authorities and other social landlords (including housing associations) can use 'right to repair' schemes to claim compensation for repairs which the landlord does not carry out within a set timescale.

Local authority tenants have a right to repair scheme which they must follow. Under the scheme, if repairs are not carried out within a fixed time scale, you can notify your landlord that you want a different contractor to do the job. The local authority must appoint a new contractor and set another time limit. You can then claim compensation if the repair is not carried out within the new time limit.

As a local authority tenant, you can currently use the 'right to repair' scheme for repairs which your landlord estimates would cost up to £250. You can also claim up to £50 compensation. Twenty types of repairs qualify for the scheme, including insecure doors, broken entry phone systems, blocked sinks and leaking roofs.

A repair will not qualify for the scheme if the local authority has fewer than 100 properties, is not responsible for the repair or if the authority decides it would cost more than £250.

If you're the tenant of another social landlord, such as a housing association, you are entitled to compensation if you report a repair or maintenance problem which affects your health, safety or security and your landlord fails twice to make the repair within the set timescale.

There is a flat rate award which is currently £10, plus £2 a day up to a total of £50, for each day the repair remains outstanding. A maximum cost for an eligible repair may be set by the individual landlord.

Improvements

As a local authority tenant if you make certain improvements to your home, for example, loft insulation, draught proofing, new baths, basins and toilets and security measures, you can apply for compensation for doing so when you move out. You will not be eligible for this compensation if you buy your home.

Disabled tenants

If you are disabled, you may be able to have alterations carried out to your home. You may first have to get the need for any alterations assessed by the social services department. Alterations could include the installation of a stair lift or hoist or adaptation of a bathroom or toilet.

If you want to get an alteration carried out you should consult an experienced adviser, for example, at a Citizens Advice Bureau.

A disabled tenant may also be able to get a disabled facilities grant to make the home more suitable.

Gas appliances

Your landlord must make sure that any gas appliances in residential premises are safe. They must arrange for safety checks on appliances and fittings to be carried out at least once every twelve months. The inspection must be carried out by someone who is registered with Gas Safety Register. Their website is: www.gassaferegister.co.uk. The landlord must also keep a record of the date of the check, any problems identified and any action taken. As the tenant, you have the right to see this record as long as you give reasonable notice.

If your landlord does not arrange for checks or refuses to allow you to see the record of the check, you could contact the local Health and Safety Executive office.

The right to stay in the accommodation

This is an outline of the rights you have as a tenant of a local authority, housing association or housing co-operative to stay in your accommodation and how you can be evicted.

Secure tenants

As a secure tenant you have the right to stay in the accommodation as long as you keep to the terms of the tenancy agreement with your landlord. However, if the tenancy agreement is broken, for example, because of rent arrears or nuisance to neighbours, your landlord can serve a notice on you and apply to the county court for eviction.

A social housing landlord can only evict you if they give you the proper notice and if one of the 'grounds for possession' applies.

What constitutes 'grounds for possession' is complicated and someone whose landlord is seeking eviction should consult an experienced adviser, for example, at a Citizens Advice Bureau.

. The landlord must apply to the county court to seek possession of the property and a secure tenant can only be evicted if the court grants a possession order to the landlord.

Assured tenants

As an assured tenant you have the right to stay in the accommodation as long as you keep to the terms of the tenancy agreement with your landlord. However, if the tenancy agreement is broken, for example, because of rent arrears or nuisance to neighbours, your landlord can serve a notice on you.

The housing association will then have to obtain a possession order from the county court by proving that one of the 'grounds for possession' applies. We discussed grounds for possession earlier in the book.

Social housing tenancies and discrimination

When renting accommodation from a local authority, housing association or other social landlord, they must not discriminate against you because of your disability, gender reassignment, pregnancy and maternity, race, religion or belief, sex or sexual orientation. This means that they are not allowed to:

- rent a property to you on worse terms than other tenants
- treat you differently from other tenants in the way you are allowed to use facilities such as a laundry or a garden
- evict or harass you because of discrimination
- charge you higher rent than other tenants
- refuse to re-house you because of discrimination
- refuse to carry out repairs to your home because of disrimination
- refuse to make reasonable changes to a property or a term in the tenancy agreement which would allow a disabled person to live there.

If you think your landlord is discriminating against you, you should get advice from an experienced adviser, for example, at a Citizens Advice Bureau.

Introductory tenants

Who is an introductory tenant?

Some local authorities make all new tenants introductory tenants for the first 12 months of the tenancy.

Rights of introductory tenants

Introductory tenants have some but not all of the rights of secure tenants. The following table shows your rights as an introductory tenant compared with secure tenants.

Statutory right	Secure tenant	Introductory tenant
Right to succession by partners or in some cases family members	yes	yes
Right to repair	yes	yes
Right to assign	yes	no
Right to buy	yes	no, but period spent as an introductory tenant counts towards the discount
Right to take in lodgers	yes	no
Right to sub-let part of your home	yes	no
Right to do improvements	yes	no
Right to exchange your home with certain other tenants	yes	no
Right to vote prior to transfer to new landlord	yes	no
Right to be consulted on housing management issues	yes	yes
Right to be consulted on decision to delegate housing management	yes	yes
Right to participate in housing management contract monitoring	yes	yes

Ending an introductory tenancy

At the end of the twelve months, provided there have been no possession proceedings against you, the introductory tenancy will usually be converted by your landlord to a secure tenancy. However, your landlord may decide to extend the introductory tenancy for a further six months. If this happens, you will be told the reasons for the decision and given the chance to ask for the decision to be reviewed.

Possession proceedings

It is very easy for a landlord to evict an introductory tenant. If you have received a notice from the landlord stating that they intend to evict you and take possession of the property, you should immediately consult an experienced adviser, for example, at a Citizens Advice Bureau.

Flexible tenants

Flexible tenancies are a type of tenancy that can be granted by local authority landlords in England, from 1 April 2012. Not all local authorities offer them.

A flexible tenancy is similar to a local authority secure tenancy. However, a secure tenancy is periodic, which means that it lasts for an indefinite period of time. Periodic tenancies are often called 'lifetime tenancies'. In contrast, a flexible tenancy lasts for a fixed period of time. In most cases, a flexible tenancy will last for at least five years.

A local authority has to serve a written notice on you before a flexible tenancy can start. The notice must tell you that the tenancy you're being offered is a flexible tenancy, and what the terms of the tenancy are.

Flexible tenants have a number of legal rights, many of which are similar to the rights of secure tenants. For example, the right to pass on your tenancy when you're alive or when you die, the right to exchange your home with certain other tenants, and the right to buy your home.

A local authority doesn't have to grant you another tenancy when the fixed term of the flexible tenancy comes to an end. You can ask the local authority to review its decision not to grant you another tenancy. The review will consider if your landlord has followed its policies and procedures when making that decision.

If you are not given another tenancy when your flexible tenancy comes to an end, the local authority will take action to evict you.

Right-to-buy.

Perhaps the most valuable right enjoyed by a secure tenant is the right to buy either the freehold, in the case of a house, or the leasehold, in the case of a flat. In order to claim this right there is also a residence qualification to fulfill. The tenant, or the tenants spouse must have been resident as a secure tenant (not necessarily in the same property) for five years prior to the application to buy.

Discounts

If you qualify for Right to Buy, you can get a discount on the market value of your home when you buy it.

The maximum discount is £75,000 across England, except in London boroughs where it's £100,000.

The discount is based on:

- how long you've been a tenant with a public sector landlord
- the type of property you're buying (a flat or a house)
- the value of your home

If you're buying with someone else, you count the years of whoever's been a public sector tenant the longest.

You'll usually have to repay some or all your discount if you sell your home within 5 years.

The discount you get might be reduced if you've used Right to Buy in the past.

Working out the discount

There are different discount levels for houses and flats.

For houses you get a 35% discount if you've been a public sector tenant for 5 years. For every extra year you've been a public sector tenant, the discount goes up by 1%, up to a maximum of 60% – or £75,000 across England and £100,000 in London boroughs (whichever is lower). .

For flats you get a 50% discount if you've been a public sector tenant for 5 years. For every extra year you've been a public sector tenant, the discount goes up by 2%, up to a maximum of 70% – or £75,000 across England and £100,000 in London boroughs (whichever is lower).

If your landlord has spent money on your home

Your discount will be less if your landlord has spent money building or maintaining your home:

- in the last 10 years - if your landlord built or acquired your home before 2 April 2012
- in the last 15 years - if you are buying your home through Preserved Right to Buy, or if your landlord acquired your home after 2 April 2012

If your landlord has spent more money than your home is now worth, you won't get any discount.

Social HomeBuy

If you can't afford to buy your home through Right to Buy, you may still be able to buy a share of it through social homebuy. With Social HomeBuy, you buy a share of your council or housing association home and pay rent on the rest of it.

Discounts

You'll get a discount of between £9,000 and £16,000 on the value of your home, depending on:

- where your home is
- the size of the share you're buying

If you want to buy another share in your home later on, you'll get a discount on that too.

Buying more of your home later

You must buy at least 25% of your home. You can buy more later, until you own 100%. This is called 'staircasing'.

If you buy more of your home, your rent will go down - because it's based on how much of the property you rent. Your landlord can charge rent of up to 3% of the value of their share of your home, per year.

ExampleYour home is worth £240,000 and you buy a 50% share. Your landlord charges you 3% rent on their 50% share. 3% of £120,000 is £3,600 per year. This works out at £300 per month for you to pay in rent.

Who can't apply

You can't use Social HomeBuy if:

- you have an assured shorthold tenancy
- you're being made bankrupt
- a court has ordered you to leave your home
- your landlord is taking action against you for rent arrears, anti-social behaviour or for breaking your tenancy agreement

Not all local councils or housing associations have joined the scheme. Check with your landlord to find out if they belong to the scheme and whether your home is included.

Rights to succeed to a secure tenancy

The tenancy does not end with the death of a secure or assured tenant. If there is a spouse then he/she will succeed to the tenancy subject to having been resident for 1 year, occupying as an only or principal home, prior to the application to succeed.

The courts have held that only persons of the opposite sex can be defined as spouse. However, this ruling may certainly be challenged in the European Court of Human Rights.

Where there is no spouse as defined then a member of the family can succeed, again with the residence qualification in place. If a family cannot decide who should succeed then the local authority or body granting the secure tenancy can make a final decision.

Only one succession is allowed and, on the death of the successor, the local authority can terminate the tenancy through formal procedures and re-let to whom it wishes.

13

PRIVATE TENANCIES IN SCOTLAND

The law governing the relationship between private landlords and tenants in Scotland is different to that in England. Since the beginning of 1989, new private sector tenancies in Scotland have been covered by the Housing (Scotland) Act 1988. Following the passage of this Act, private sector tenants no longer have any protection as far as rent levels are concerned and tenants enjoy less security of tenure.

There are four essential elements in the creation of a tenancy under Scottish law:

- An agreement between landlord and tenant
- The payment of rent. If someone is allowed to occupy a property without an agreement then this will not amount to a tenancy
- A fixed permission date (called an 'ish')
- Possession

The agreement must be in writing if the tenancy is for a period of 1 year or more. Agreements of less than a year can be oral.

Protected tenancies

Before 1989, most private sector tenancies were likely to be protected tenancies. A protected tenancy is a contractual tenancy covered by the Rent Act (Scotland) 1984 and must satisfy the following requirements:

- The house must be let as a dwelling house (this can apply to a house or part of a house)
- The house must be a separate dwelling
- The ratable value must be less than a specified sum

Various categories of dwellings did not qualify as protected tenancies. A protected tenancy retains its status until the death of a tenant or his or her spouse, or any eligible successor, and therefore some protected tenancies are still in existence today.

Grounds for possession

As is the case in England and Wales, where there is no protected tenancy, the landlord may possess a property only by obtaining a court order. The landlord must serve a notice to quit, giving 28 days notice. A ground for possession must be shown, either discretionary or mandatory before possession can be given.

The grounds for possession are similar to those in England and Wales, with ten mandatory and ten discretionary grounds applying.

Fair rent system

A fair rent system, similar to England and Wales, exists in Scotland for protected tenants. There is a set procedure to be followed, with either the landlord or tenant, or jointly, making an application to the rent officer. Once fixed, the rent is valid for three years. A fresh application can be made within three years if circumstances relating to the tenancy radically alter, such as a substantial refurbishment.

Assured tenants

Under the Housing (Scotland) Act 1988, the assured tenancy was introduced into Scotland coming into force after 2nd January 1989. This is very similar indeed to the assured tenancy introduced into England and Wales in 1989.

A Scottish assured tenancy has three elements:

- the tenancy must be of a house or flat or self contained dwelling. For an agreement to exist, there must be an agreement, rent payable a termination date and possession, as there is in all leases in Scotland
- The house must be let as a separate dwelling. A tenancy may be of a flat, part of a house, or even a single room, provided it is possible for the

tenant to carry on all 'the major activities of residential life there, i.e. sleeping, cooking and feeding'.

- The tenant must be an individual. A company cannot be given an assured tenancy

The list of exclusions from assured tenancy status are the same as those in England and all the other provisions concerning rent, sub-letting succession, security of tenure and so on, apply.

The grounds for possession and the law governing termination of tenancies is a reflection of English Law.

Short assured tenancies

The Housing Act (Scotland) also introduced 'short assured tenancies', a distinct form of assured tenancy for a fixed term of six months. Again, this is a reflection of the assured shorthold with the same provisions applying.

14

THE LAW AND OWNER OCCUPIERS COMMONHOLD, FREEHOLD AND LEASEHOLD

Commonhold and Leasehold Reform Act 2002

The Commonhold and Leasehold Reform Act 2002 introduced into English law an entirely new form of tenure, namely commonhold. It is specifically targeted at blocks of flats, where leasehold has been the normal form of tenure until now. We will discuss commonhold briefly a little later, suffice to say that with such an arrangement in a block of flats the commonholders own all the common parts together with leases being abolished.

Freehold and Leasehold

The law does not look at property in the same way as most lay people. Most people think in terms of houses and other buildings; the law is more interested in the land beneath. A freehold home owner will say "I own my house." But the law will say "He owns the land on which is built the house he lives in." To the law, the key point is that he owns the land - the buildings on it are incidental.

For practical purposes, the strongest form of title to land is that of freehold. Freehold title lasts forever; it may be bought and sold, or passed by inheritance. In short, freehold title is tantamount to outright ownership, and is taken as such for the purposes of this book.

Freeholders may, of course, use their land for their own purposes. The freehold home owner is merely the most familiar example. But they may also, if they wish, allow other people to use their land. And this is where leases, and other forms of tenure, come in.

Suppose you would like to make use of a piece of land owned by someone else. The owner is unwilling to sell it to you, but, having no immediate use for it himself, is willing to allow you to use it for a time, perhaps in exchange for payment. At its simplest, this arrangement implies no more than a licence - the owner's (i.e. landlord's) permission for you to be on his land.

But such a licence can be revoked by the landlord at any time, with or without a good reason. As such it is not very valuable, so if the owner wants to make money by allowing other people to use his land, he needs to give them a legal status that they will be willing to pay for. This is achieved by granting a lease or tenancy. It should be noted here that, from the legal point of view, a lease and a tenancy are the same thing; but in practice, the terms tend to be used in different contexts. This is explained below: for the present, we shall call it a lease.

A lease grants the leaseholder permission to use the land for a certain period, which can be anything from a day or two to several thousand years. It will usually attach conditions, for example that the leaseholder must pay rent (usually a sum of money, although in principle other goods or services could constitute rent).

The lease may, but does not have to, put certain restrictions on what the leaseholder may do with the land. But it must, in order to be a lease rather than merely a licence, grant the leaseholder 'exclusive possession'. This is the right to exclude other people, especially the landlord, from the land. Such a right need not be absolute, and exceptions to it are explained later in the book: but it is enough to give the leaseholder a high degree of control over the land, which has become, for the duration of the lease, very much the leaseholder's land rather than the freeholder's. A lease, unless it contains a stipulation to the contrary, may be bought, sold, or inherited; if this happens, all the rights and duties under it pass to the new owner.

Leases and Tenancies

Confusion is often caused by the fact that, although the terms leaseholder (or lessee) and tenant are legally interchangeable, they tend to be used in different senses. The tendency is to refer to short leases as tenancies: the more substantial the rights conferred, and the longer the period for which they run, the likelier it is that the agreement will be referred to as a lease. For the purposes of this book, an agreement will be referred to as a 'tenancy' if it is periodic or runs for a fixed term of less than seven years. A fixed term agreement running for more than seven years will be referred to as a 'lease'.

A 'periodic' tenancy is one that runs from period to period (usually, from week to week or month to month) until something intervenes to stop it, and is conditional on payment of rent. A tenancy that runs for a fixed term of less than seven years has a definite date of expiry but is otherwise similar to a periodic tenancy and will depend on regular payment of rent. Tenancies granted by local authorities and housing associations tend to be periodic; private landlords generally grant either periodic tenancies or short fixed-term tenancies (typically, six months). At any rate, the landlord of a periodic or short-term tenancy will usually accept most of the responsibility for maintaining the property and will charge a relatively high rent to allow for this. If the tenancy is for residential property, the landlord's duty to maintain the dwelling is imposed by law (Landlord and Tenant Act 1985).

It is common for private landlords to insist on prepayment of rent or a deposit before granting a tenancy, and many landlords will levy a separate service charge to cover the cost of some activities that are peripheral to the central one of providing housing; but despite these costs it would be true to say that the principal financial responsibility accepted by a periodic or short-term tenant is that of paying the rent.

The position of a leaseholder is very different. The major financial commitment will usually be a substantial initial payment either to the landlord (if the lease is newly created) or to the previous leaseholder. There is still a rent, called a ground rent, payable to the landlord, but it is usually a notional amount (£50 or £100 a year is not uncommon). Its purpose is not so much to give the landlord an income as to give the leaseholder an annual reminder that ultimate ownership of the land is not his.

Types of Leasehold Property

In the context of residential property, it should be noted that the great majority of leases relate to flats rather than houses. This is because of the legal concept of land tenure as described above. If a builder buys some freehold land and covers it in houses, it is possible to parcel out the area so that each bit of freehold land, and the house standing on it, can be sold separately. It does not matter if the houses are semi-detached or terraced, because there is well-established law governing party walls of adjoining freeholders. But if there are flats, the builder has a problem: how can the flats be sold since they cannot be said to stand on separate and distinct bits of land? The answer is to sell leases.

Where flats are sold, each purchaser acquires a lease that gives him specified rights over the parcel of land on which the flats stand. These rights, of course, are shared by the leaseholders of the other flats. In addition, however, each leaseholder gains the right to exclusive possession of part of the building occupying the land - his own flat. The leaseholder would say "I own my flat", but the law says "He owns a lease granting him certain rights, in particular that of access, to a defined parcel of land and the right of exclusive possession of specified parts of a building erected on that land." This may seem a slightly unusual way of looking at it, but it is fundamental to understanding the way that the law sees the relationship between leaseholders of flats and their freeholders.

The freehold of flatted property will often be retained by the developer, although sometimes it will be sold to a property company. Formerly, it was common practice for the freehold to be retained even when separate houses were built. This allowed the freeholder to retain an interest in the property and, above all, to regain full possession of it when the lease expired. However, the position of freeholders has been weakened by three key pieces of legislation, the Leasehold Reform Act 1967, the Leasehold Reform, Housing and Urban Development Act 1993, and the Commonhold and Leasehold Reform Act 2002. These Acts are described in detail further on: their overall effect is to entitle leaseholders either to the freehold of houses or to a new lease of flats. In view of the legislation, there is now little point in the original owner's attempting to retain the freehold of land on which houses have been built. The exception is where a house is sold on the basis of shared ownership - see below.

Most residential leasehold property therefore consists of flats. Of these, most are in the private sector, comprising purpose-built blocks and (especially in London) conversions of what were once large single houses. The freehold will usually belong to the developer, to a property company, or sometimes to the original owner of the site.

House leases normally give most of the repairing responsibility to the leaseholder - services provided by the freeholder, and therefore service charges, are minimal. In flats, however, although the leaseholder will normally be responsible for the interior of the flat, the freeholder will maintain the fabric of the building and will recoup the costs of doing so by levying service charges on the leaseholders. This is an area of such potential conflict between leaseholders and freeholders that it has been the subject of legislation. It is dealt with fully further on in the book.

Mixed-tenure blocks: the right to buy

The general shift from renting to owning means that sometimes flats have been sold in blocks that were originally developed for letting to tenants: the result is often a 'mixed-tenure' block, with both leaseholders and tenants. Although this sometimes happens in the private sector, it is particularly common in blocks owned by local authorities and housing associations, for it is to these that the statutory right to buy applies. This right was created by the Housing Act 1980 and allows most local authority tenants, and some housing association tenants, to buy their homes at a heavily discounted price. Tenants of houses are normally sold the freehold, but tenants of flats become leaseholders.

Shared ownership

Another result of the trend towards home ownership has been the dramatic expansion of shared ownership. This is a form of tenure that combines leasing and renting. However, the term 'shared ownership' is something of a misnomer because ownership is not, in fact, shared between the leaseholder and the freeholder. The lease relates to the whole property, not part of it, and the shared owner is as entitled as any other leaseholder to consider himself the owner of his house. The key point about shared ownership leases is not that they give an inferior form of tenure to other leases but that they have different conditions attached. The leaseholder pays less than the full value of the lease; typically, half. In exchange for this concession, he pays not the normal notional ground rent but a much more substantial rent. However, he is much more a leaseholder than he is a tenant, and, like other leaseholders (but unlike tenants) is responsible for the internal repair of the property and, in the case of houses, usually the fabric of the building too.

Shared owners usually have the right to increase their stake as and when they can afford it: this is called 'staircasing' because the owner's share goes up in steps. If the property is a house, the freehold will normally be transferred when the owner's share reaches 100%, and he will then be in the same position as any other freehold home owner. If it is a flat, he will continue to be a leaseholder but there will no longer be a rental (other than ground rent).

Head Leases and Subleases

For the sake of clarity and brevity, this book has been written throughout on the basis that there are only two parties involved: the freeholder and the leaseholder. Usually this picture is accurate; but it is the right of the leaseholder, unless the lease specifically forbids it, to sublet the property, or part of it, to someone else. This means that the leaseholder delegates some of his rights over the property to another person. Obviously, he cannot delegate rights greater than his own, so that if he holds a lease of the property running until 2025 he cannot grant a sublease running until 2050. And he cannot grant a sublease of the whole of his rights because this would leave him with no interest in the property: it would, in fact, amount to the same as an assignment. So it is necessary for a sublease that the original leaseholder be left with something; either some period of time or some part of the property.

It is possible in theory to have a whole hierarchy of leases applying to a particular property, starting with the freehold, then the head lease, then a sublease, followed by sub-subleases and possibly sub-sub-subleases below those. There are two rules that limit this kind of proliferation: one, explained above, is that each lease must confer less, in space or time or both, than the one above it; and the other, that is a lease may not be held by the same person as holds the lease (or freehold) immediately above it.

Commonhold

To try to deal with problems arising from the relationship between freeholders and leaseholders, a new form of tenure, 'commonhold', was created by the Commonhold and Leasehold Reform Act 2002. It is designed specifically for use in blocks of flats, and the idea is that all the individual flat owners (or 'unit holders', as the Act calls them) will belong to a 'commonhold association', a registered company that operate under a constitution (the 'memorandum and articles') and act in accordance with a 'commonhold community statement'. This arrangement ensures that each unit holder will have two separate interests in relation to the property: individually, and collectively, in the block as a whole.

15

OBLIGATIONS OF FREEHOLDER AND LEASEHOLDER

General Principles

For centuries the law did little to regulate the relationship between freeholders and leaseholders. The view was taken that they had entered into the relationship of their own free will, and it was up to them to agree whatever terms and conditions they liked. If either party did not keep the bargain, he could of course be sued in the courts, but, on the whole, the law did not interfere in the bargain itself.

In the twentieth century, however, the view grew up that some types of bargain are inherently unfair and even those that are not might still be open to exploitation.

An example of the first type is an agreement that residential property will revert to the original freeholder at the end of a long lease. This meant that when 99-year leases expired, leaseholders found that their homes had abruptly returned to the outright ownership of the heir of the original freeholder, leaving them as mere trespassers liable to be ejected at any time. In practice, freeholders were usually willing to grant a fresh lease, but sometimes only at a very high price that the leaseholder might well be unable to afford. In some cases, freeholders insisted on reclaiming the property however much the leaseholder offered, and the law supported them. This is the state of affairs that led to legislation entitling almost all residential leaseholders to extend their leases, and many of them to claim the freehold.

The freeholder's right to demand a service charge is an example of an arrangement that is fair in principle but open to abuse in practice. It is inevitable, especially in flats, that responsibility for some types of repair cannot be ascribed to any individual leaseholder and must therefore be retained by the freeholder; who must, in turn, recoup the cost from leaseholders. However, some freeholders abused this system by levying extravagant service charges that made the service charge a source of profit. To prevent this, there is now a substantial body of legislation designed to ensure that freeholders carry out only the works that are really necessary and that they recover their legitimate costs and no more. The complicated rules governing this are chiefly found in the Landlord and Tenant Act 1985 (as amended) and are described in Chapter Three.

Under the Landlord and Tenant Act 1987, either party to a long lease (one originally granted for at least 21 years) may go to the Leasehold Valuation Tribunal (or 'LVT') to argue that the lease is deficient in some way and needs to be changed. If only the one lease is affected, the tribunal may vary it. Sometimes, however, a number of leases may need to be changed; in this case either the freeholder or 75% of the leaseholders may apply.

Obligations of Leaseholders

The obligations of leaseholders are set out in the lease; indeed, since it is a document drafted by or on behalf of freeholders, one of its main aims is to tell leaseholders what they must and must not do. However, legislation and judicial decisions sometimes come to the leaseholder's assistance.

Consumer legislation can also apply to leases; in particular, the Unfair Terms in Consumer Contracts Regulations 1999 (which replace earlier regulations made in 1995) have a major impact. These apply to standard terms in contracts. This means they normally cover the terms of leases, which are usually presented to potential leaseholders as a package with no opportunity to renegotiate individual terms. Occasionally, however, individual terms can be specifically negotiated and it should be noted that in that case the Unfair Terms Regulations do not apply. Nor will they apply to any lease granted before the earlier version of the regulations which came in July 1995. The Office of Fair Trading has issued advice about the types of term that are likely to be judged unfair in the context of assured tenancies. The OFT has not issued advice about long leases, but it is likely that similar standards would apply.

a: Plain and intelligible language
Over many years property lawyers have developed an obscure and technical language that can have the effect of excluding outsiders. This form of

'legalese' is characterised by unwieldy sentences with few (or no) commas to break them up, long lists often consisting of different names for the same thing, and a vocabulary of unfamiliar words and (worst of all) familiar words given unfamiliar meanings.

For instance, in normal English the verb 'determine' means 'ascertain' or 'firmly decide', but when a property lawyer applies it to a lease it means 'end' or 'terminate' (as in 'the lease shall determine if...'). Property lawyers also have a well-merited reputation for using words like 'hereinafter' and 'aforesaid', which, although not ambiguous, are hardly everyday English, while occasional outbreaks of Latin are not unknown (*pari passu* and *mutatis mutandis*).

Thankfully, this style is going out of fashion and an increasing number of modern leases are being written in more intelligible language, and for leases made since 1995 the Unfair Terms Regulations mean that arcanely written terms may be unenforceable. However, a huge number of leases written in traditional style still have decades or even centuries to run, so unfortunately property lawyers' English will be with us for a long time yet.

b: Terms Unfair on Consumers

There are some terms to which the Office of Fair Trading objects in any consumer contract. These are terms that place an unreasonable burden on the customer (the leaseholder) or give an unfair advantage to the supplier (the freeholder). Some of these terms are common in long leases.

There may be a clause in which the leaseholder declares that he has 'read and understood' the lease, even though the document is long and complex and it unlikely that anyone would read (or understand) the whole of it. The aim is to put the leaseholder at a disadvantage in any dispute by arguing that he was fully aware of all the terms of the lease. Another way of loading the scales is a clause allowing the freeholder the final decision about vital matters, such as whether or not the freeholder and the leaseholder have fulfilled their respective obligations under the lease.

These clauses are probably unenforceable in leases made since July 1995, but in earlier leases they are probably valid.

There are other types of clause that are potentially a problem for the leaseholder. An example is a clause laying down procedural formalities. Such a clause is not necessarily a problem: for instance, leases commonly require formal communications between the freeholder and the leaseholder to be in writing, and this is a perfectly reasonable requirement because it reduces the chances misunderstandings or disputes about who said what. But it is harder to justify a requirement for notices to be sent by registered post, and some leases stipulate procedures that are so onerous that the aim seems to be to deter leaseholders from exercising their rights.

Similar comments apply to clauses imposing financial penalties for breaches of the lease. This is not necessarily unreasonable, but sometimes the penalties are out of all proportion to the nature of the breach.

Some leases require the leaseholder to join with the freeholder (and help with the cost) in responding to legal or other notices pertaining to the property. Again, this may be reasonable in some circumstances, but as a blanket requirement it can act against leaseholders' interests.

An interesting and debatable issue is the prohibition of set-off, which is a standard clause in most leases. 'Set-off' is the practice of deducting (or 'setting off') from any payment made by one party under an agreement any sums that are owed by the other party. For instance, suppose a leaseholder considers that a repair to the fabric of the building is the freeholder's responsibility, but the freeholder either disputes this or fails to take any action. Eventually the leaseholder does the work at his own expense, and next time the annual service charge falls due he reimburses himself by deducting, or 'setting off', the cost from his service charge payment.

Leaseholders like set-off because it is an easy way of reclaiming disputed sums from the freeholder, and it shifts onto the freeholder the onus of continuing the dispute. Freeholders dislike it for exactly the same reasons, which is why leases normally prohibit it. The Office of Fair Trading, in its advice on assured tenancies, says that prohibiting set-off is unfair, but it is not clear whether the same advice would apply to leases.

The possibility that unfair, or potentially unfair, clauses will feature in a lease underlines the need for competent legal advice before signing it. An experienced solicitor will be able to advise whether doubtful clauses can be, or are likely to be, used against leaseholders. Leaseholders may also have remedies available under the Landlord and Tenant Act: this is covered below and, in the key area of service charges, in the next Chapter.

c: Restrictive clauses in leases

So far, we have looked at leases as if they were consumer contracts, and outlined some of the clauses they may contain that could affect leaseholders in their capacity as consumers. But there are some further potentially difficult terms that relate specifically to property issues. These terms are not necessarily unreasonable. For example, in a lease concerning an upstairs flat it would be quite normal to have a clause requiring the leaseholder to keep the premises carpeted. This makes sense because bare floors, although currently very fashionable, could be very noisy for the people in the flat below.

The Office of Fair Trading's advice identifies several types of sweeping provisions that would, if they were enforced, considerably restrict the tenant's ability to live a normal life. Although the OFT's advice relates to assured tenancies, similar objections would probably apply to these clauses in leases. For example:

- **Pets** Leases often lay down that the leaseholder may not own pets, or may not do so without the freeholder's permission.

- **Upkeep** Leases may say that the leaseholder must decorate periodically - say, every five or seven years. Where there is a garden, it is common for the leaseholder to be required to keep it in good order.

- **Business** Leases often lay down that the leaseholder must not run any sort of business from his home.

- **Use as residence** A lease will generally say that the property is to be used for the residential purposes of the leaseholder and his household, and that it cannot be sublet. It will sometimes attempt to restrict how many people may live there apart from the leaseholder.

- **Other** Leases sometimes forbid such things as the keeping of flammable materials and the installation of television aerials or satellite dishes. They may require leaseholders to drain hot water systems whenever they are away, or keep the premises clean and free of dust.

It is easy to see why freeholders want such clauses in the lease: it is because they realise that there will be serious problems if someone attempts, for instance, to keep four alsatians in a studio flat. The neighbours will be inconvenienced and will complain to the freeholder, and leases of other flats in the same block will become difficult to sell.

The same arguments could apply if one of the leaseholders allows his flat to fall into complete decorative decay or if he runs a noisy and busy trade from his home.

But the kind of blanket rules that appear in many leases go too far. A rule against any pets at all forbids not only four noisy alsatians but also entirely inoffensive pets such as a budgie or a goldfish. In the same way, prohibiting business activities means that the leaseholder may not use his home to write a book for publication, or address envelopes, and so on - types of home working that could not possibly inconvenience anyone.

The rule against sub-letting also prevents leaseholders from exploiting the value of their property by letting it out, something that is open to most home-owners and is increasingly accepted as normal.

For leases made since July 1995, these sweeping clauses are probably unfair and unenforceable. But even for older leases, the reality is that such broad provisions are seldom enforced. Freeholders, and their lawyers, like them because they feel that they preserve their freedom of action, allowing them to decide whether or not to enforce the lease if it is clear that one of these blanket conditions is being broken. But there are two problems with this attitude.

The first is that it creates uncertainty in the minds of leaseholders. Suppose the leases in a block of flats prohibit all pets, but leaseholder A has a goldfish and no action has been taken even though the freeholder is aware of the infringement. Leaseholder B may well conclude that there will be no objection if he gets a cat. If still there is no action, leaseholder C may feel able to get a couple of dogs - and so on. So the fact that restrictions are so broad can have the paradoxical effect of reducing their effectiveness.

The second problem is that if, in the example just given, the freeholder takes legal action to force C to get rid of the dogs, it is possible that C will argue in court that the treatment of the other leaseholders shows that the freeholder is not seriously interested in banning pets and that the action has been motivated rather by petty spite or bias.

It would be better if freeholders and their lawyers drafted leases that say what they mean: not that leaseholders may have no pets at all, but that they may have no pets apt to damage the property or cause inconvenience or annoyance to other persons. The same principle should apply to clauses dealing with sub-letting or working from home.

It is unfortunate that this book is forced to advise leaseholders to ignore some parts of their leases. The responsibility for this, however, lies with freeholders and their lawyers for writing into standard leases blanket conditions purporting to prohibit entirely inoffensive behaviour. This practice makes it inevitable, in the real world that leaseholders will disregard certain clauses, and that books like this will have to give them some indication of when they can probably do so safely. Most leaseholders exercise common sense and realise that the freeholder is unlikely to take action unless there is a complaint, which means that the leaseholder may do almost whatever he pleases provided he refrains from provoking anyone. It is sensible to stay on good terms with neighbours to ensure that if anything is bothering them they take it up directly with you rather than report the matter to the freeholder. Other leaseholders will also be able to tell you what view has been taken in the past - both by other residents and by the freeholder - in doubtful cases.

d: Restrictions on sale

Some leases restrict the kind of person to whom the lease may be sold (or 'assigned' - see below). For example, a housing scheme may have been intended specifically for the elderly. Clearly, it will not be maintained as such if leaseholders are free to assign or bequeath their leases to whomever they please, so the lease will say that it may be assigned only to persons above a certain age, and that if it is inherited by anyone outside the age group it must be sold on to someone qualified to hold it. Although this could be described as an onerous term because it makes it more difficult to find a buyer and may reduce the lease's value, it is reasonable given the need to ensure that the scheme continues to house elderly people exclusively. And the restriction it imposes is not too severe because so many potential purchasers qualify.

However, some leases define much more narrowly to whom they may be sold. Sometimes the freeholder is a body owned and run by the leaseholders themselves, and in these cases it is usual to require that all leaseholders must join the organisation and, if they leave it, must immediately dispose of the lease to someone that is willing to join. Again, such a term is not necessarily unacceptable. If the organisation makes relatively light demands on its members (perhaps no more than a modest admission fee or annual subscription), the restriction is unlikely greatly to diminish the value of the lease. If, however, the organisation expects much more from its members - perhaps that they actively take part in running it, or that they pay a large annual subscription - the value of the lease will be severely reduced because it will be difficult to find purchasers willing to accept the conditions. A key point is whether the organisation has power to expel members, thus forcing them to sell; and, if so, in what circumstances and by whom this power can be exercised.

e: Access

Virtually any lease will contain a clause allowing the freeholder to enter the property in order to inspect or repair it. This has the effect of qualifying the leaseholder's right of exclusive possession (see below), but only subject to certain conditions. The freeholder (or the freeholder's servants, such as agents or contractors) may enter only at reasonable times, and subject to the giving of reasonable notice. If these conditions are not met, the leaseholder is under no obligation to allow them in; and, even when the conditions are met, the landlord will be trespassing if he enters the property without the leaseholder's consent. If the leaseholder refuses consent even though the time is reasonable and reasonable notice has been given, the landlord's remedy is to get a court order against the leaseholder compelling him to grant entry. It is probable, in such a case, that the landlord will seek, and get, an award of legal costs against the leaseholder.

f: Arbitration

Many leases contain clauses providing that disputes can be submitted to arbitration at the request of either party. By the Commonhold and Leasehold Reform Act, the effect of these clauses is limited, because the results will not be binding so far as the Leasehold Valuation Tribunal is concerned. If, however, once a dispute has arisen, the parties to agree to submit it to an agreed arbitrator, they are bound by the result, which is enforceable by the courts. If such a 'post-dispute' arbitration finds that the leaseholder is in breach, this is equivalent to a finding by the LVT and will (if the other requirements are met) allow the freeholder to proceed with forfeiture. Arbitration may be a useful mechanism in some cases, and it may be cheaper and quicker than legal action, but it may be difficult to find an arbitrator in whom both parties have confidence.

Obligations of Freeholders
a: Exclusive possession and quiet enjoyment
The first and most important obligation on the freeholder, without which there would be no legal lease at all, is to respect the leaseholder's rights of 'exclusive possession' and 'quiet enjoyment'. Exclusive possession is the right to occupy the property and exclude others from it, especially the freeholder. Quiet enjoyment is another way of underlining the leaseholder's rights over the property: it means that the freeholder may not interfere with the leaseholder's use of the property provided that the terms of the lease are observed.

However, the leaseholder's right to quiet enjoyment applies only to breaches by the freeholder or the freeholder's servants such as agents or contractors. It is important to note this because the term is sometimes thought to mean that the freeholder must protect the leaseholder against any activity by anyone that interferes with his use of the property: this is not so. For example, if the freeholder carries out some activity elsewhere in the building that interferes with the leaseholder, the leaseholder's right to quiet enjoyment has been breached and he is entitled to redress unless the freeholder can show that the activity was necessary, for instance to comply with repairing obligations under the lease. But if the interference is caused by someone else, perhaps another leaseholder, the freeholder's obligation to provide quiet enjoyment has not been breached. And it is worth stressing in this connection that even if the other leaseholder is in breach of his lease, it is entirely up to the freeholder whether or not to take action: other leaseholders have no power to force the freeholder to deal with the situation.

This means that if one leaseholder is breaking his lease by holding noisy parties late at night, the other leaseholders may ask, but may not require, the freeholder to take action to enforce the lease. They may, however, take legal action directly against the offending leaseholder for nuisance.

b: The 'section 48' notice

Another important protection for leaseholders is found in section 48 of the Landlord and Tenant Act 1987. This was designed to deal with the situation in which freeholders seek to avoid their responsibilities by (to put it bluntly) doing a disappearing act. Sometimes freeholders would provide no address or telephone number or other means of contact, meaning that leaseholders were unable to hold the freeholder to his side of the agreement. Sections 47 and 48 therefore lay down that the freeholder must formally notify the leaseholder of his name and give an address within England and Wales at which he can be contacted, and that this information must be repeated on every demand for rent or service charge. This has proved especially valuable for leaseholders where the freeholder lives abroad, or is a company based abroad. It should be noted that the address does not have to be the freeholder's home, nor, if the freeholder is a company, its registered office; often it will be the address of a solicitor or property management company, or simply an accommodation address. But the key point is that any notice, or legal writ, is validly served if sent to that address, and the freeholder is not allowed to claim that it never came to his notice.

It is not necessary for the notice required by section 48 to be given in a separate document; it is enough if the name and address is clearly given as part of some other document such as a service charge demand. But if the necessary notice is not given, no payment of rent, service charge, or anything else is due to the freeholder; the leaseholder may lawfully withhold it until section 48 is complied with. But leaseholders withholding payments on this ground must be careful; once the notice is given, it has retrospective effect, so that all the money due to the freeholder then becomes due immediately. Any leaseholder withholding money on the grounds that section 48 has not been complied with should, therefore, make sure that he has the money easily available so that he can pay up if he has to.

c: Good management

The freeholder is under an obligation to ensure that his management responsibilities are carried out in a proper and appropriate way. Leaseholders can challenge the freeholder in court or at the LVT if they believe they can show that they are not receiving the standard of management to which they are entitled. This may be an expensive and lengthy process but it better than the alternative, sometimes resorted to by leaseholders, of withholding rent or service charge. This is risky because, whatever the shortcomings of the freeholder's management, it puts the leaseholders in breach of the conditions of their lease and, as such, demonstrably in the wrong (even if the freeholder may be in the wrong as well).

Withholding due payments is therefore not recommended unless the freeholder is so clearly at fault that arguably no payment is due - for instance, if the service being charged for has clearly not been provided at all (as opposed to being provided inadequately), or if there has been no 'section 48' notice (see above). If leaseholders choose to withhold payment, they are strongly advised to keep the money readily to hand so that they can pay up at once if the freeholder rectifies the problem; the danger otherwise is that they will be taken to court and required to pay immediately to avoid forfeiture (see below).

Powers of Leaseholders over Management

If leaseholders want a scrutiny of the standards of management of their flats, they have power under the Leasehold Reform, Housing and Urban Development Act 1993 to demand a management audit by an auditor acting on behalf of at least two-thirds of the qualifying leaseholders. Qualifying leaseholders are those with leases of residential property originally granted for 21 years or more and requiring them to contribute to the cost of services.

The purpose of the audit, the costs of which must be met by the leaseholders demanding it, is to discover whether the freeholder's duties are being carried out efficiently and effectively. The auditor is appointed by the leaseholders and must be either a qualified accountant or a qualified surveyor and must not live in the block concerned. The auditor has the right to demand papers from the freeholder and can go to court if they are not produced.

Leaseholders' Right to Manage

Leaseholders with long leases (those originally granted for 21 years or more) also have the right to take over management of their block if they wish. This applies to blocks of two or more flats (five or more if there is a resident

109

landlord) and no substantial non-residential part. It does not apply if the freeholder is a local authority.

The leaseholders must first form a 'Right to Manage' company ('RtM' company), which is a limited company whose membership is confined to leaseholders and the freeholder. Before seeking to take over management the RtM company must advise all leaseholders of its intention and invite them to participate. Fourteen days after this invitation, and provided the RtM company includes at least half the eligible tenants (or both, if only two are eligible), it can serve a claim notice on the landlord (or on the Leasehold Valuation Tribunal, if the landlord is untraceable) giving at least four months' notice of its intention to take over the management. The landlord has a month to serve a counter-notice objecting to the claim, in which case the LVT will adjudicate. If no counter-notice is served, or if the LVT so decides, the RtM company duly takes over management.

The landlord must bring to an end as quickly as possible any existing management arrangements applying to the block. The RtM company takes over the landlord's management functions, including services, repairs, maintenance, improvements, and insurance. The landlord retains its role in respect of any flats without long leaseholders (for example, those let on assured tenancies), and continues to deal with forfeiture (for more on forfeiture see the section below 'If the lease is breached'). Essentially the RtM company steps into the landlord's shoes so far as management is concerned, and it is responsible to both the landlord and the individual leaseholders for the proper carrying out of its functions.

Many leases require the landlord's approval before certain things can be done, such as assigning the lease or sub-letting. The RtM company takes over this function from the landlord, but must consult the landlord before granting approval. If the landlord objects, the matter is referred to the LVT. It seems, however, that refusal of consent by the RtM is final and cannot be challenged by the landlord (although it might be challenged by the leaseholder in question on the ground that the relevant term of the lease is unenforceable). The RtM company has authority to enforce covenants in the lease, but not by means of forfeiture.

At first blush the power to take over management in this way may appear attractive. However, leaseholders should think very carefully before they commit themselves; there are some potential snags.

The biggest problem is one of enforcement. So long as all leaseholders are agreed about what needs to be done, and are all willing and able to meet their obligations (including that of paying for services), enforcement will not be an issue and all will be well. But if some individual leaseholders refuse to pay their share, or fail to abide by the covenants in their leases, the RtM company will have to act to enforce the leases and this may well be difficult. In the first place, any steps to enforce leases will pit neighbour against neighbour and are virtually certain to cause animosity in the block. Secondly, the powerful tool of forfeiture, or threatened forfeiture, is denied to a RtM company. Finally, the RtM company, unlike most freeholders, will not have any substantial financial resources that would allow it to pursue lengthy legal action against individual leaseholders.

There are other issues. The RtM company will depend on the voluntary efforts of its members, and experience shows that many people are not willing to put in the time and effort involved in attending meetings and carrying out essential administration. RtM companies have to operate under a special constitution laid down by the Government; the aim of this is to guarantee all leaseholders' rights to be involved, but because the constitution is a standard document applying to all cases it is likely that many leaseholders will find it clumsy and inflexible. Finally, there is the question of continuing relations with the freeholder, which will expect its interests as ultimate owner to be respected by the RtM company.

In short, leaseholders contemplating the formation of a RtM company need to be sure that they are committed not only for the immediate effort of setting it up but for the long haul of carrying out management in the future. They should also recognise that, no matter how united everyone may be to start with, sooner or later the issue of enforcement will rear its head. They should certainly get legal advice about their new responsibilities before committing themselves.

The law allows another remedy in extreme cases of mismanagement. A leaseholder can use the Landlord and Tenant Act 1987 to force the appointment of a managing agent to run the block instead of the freeholder. The leaseholder must serve a notice telling the freeholder what the problems are and warning that unless they are put right a Leasehold Valuation Tribunal will be asked to appoint a managing agent. The LVT may make such an order if it satisfied that it is 'just and convenient'; the Act mentions, as specific examples where this may apply, cases where the freeholder is in breach of obligations under the lease and cases where service charges are being levied in respect of work of a poor standard or an unnecessarily high standard. Note that the procedure is not available if the freeholder is a local authority, a registered housing association, or the Crown.

Recognised Tenants' Association
A recognised tenants' association (RTA), where there is one, has additional rights to be consulted about managing agents. The RTA can serve a notice requiring the freeholder to supply details of the managing agent and the terms of the management agreement.

Leaseholders that are receiving a consistently poor or overpriced service may also wish to consider getting rid of the freeholder altogether by collective enfranchisement under the Leasehold Reform, Housing and Urban Development Act 1993.

Assignment of Leases
One of the most important characteristics of a lease - in marked contrast to most tenancies - is that it may be bought and sold. Usually, the freeholder has no say in this: the leaseholder may sell to whom he likes for the best price he can get, provided that the purchaser agrees to be bound by the terms of the lease. It is, however, usual for the lease to lay down that the freeholder must be informed of any change of leaseholder.

What actually happens when a lease is sold is that the vendor agrees to transfer to the buyer his rights and obligations under the lease. This is called 'assignment' of the lease. In some types of housing the freeholder has the right to intervene if an assignment is envisaged. The housing may, for instance, be reserved for a particular category of resident, such as the retired, so the freeholder is allowed to refuse consent to the assignment if the purchaser does not qualify.

It was mentioned above that the assignee takes over all the rights and responsibilities attaching to the lease. This means, for instance, that he takes responsibility for any arrears of service charge. This is why purchasers' solicitors go to such lengths to ensure that no arrears or other unusual obligations are outstanding.

If the Lease Is Breached

If the terms of a lease are broken, the party offended against can go to court. This may be the leaseholder, for instance if the freeholder has failed to carry out a repair. But it is normally the freeholder that takes the leaseholder to court, for failure to pay ground rent or service charges or for breach of some other requirement.

It is for the court, if satisfied that the lease has been breached, to decide what to do. The normal remedy will be that the offending party must pay compensation and that the breach (if it is still continuing) must be put right. It is also likely that the loser will be obliged to pay the winner's legal costs as well as his own, a penalty often considerably more severe that the requirement to pay compensation.

A much more severe remedy open to the freeholder if the leaseholder is in breach is forfeiture of the lease. This means what it says: the lease is forfeit to the freeholder. Forfeiture is sometimes threatened by the more aggressive class of freeholder but the good news for leaseholders is that in practice courts have shown themselves loath to grant it except in very serious cases. Since the Housing Act 1996 took effect, forfeiture for unpaid service charges has been made more difficult for freeholders; this is covered in the next Chapter.

Where forfeiture is threatened for any reason other than failure to pay rent (which, depending on the terms of the lease, may or may not include the service charge element), the freeholder must first serve a 'section 146 notice', so called after the relevant provision of the Law of Property Act 1925. In this he must state the nature of the breach of the lease, what action is required to put it right; if he wants monetary compensation for the breach, the notice must state this too.

Before the section 146 notice can be issued, it must be established that a breach of the lease has occurred. If the leaseholder has admitted the breach, the notice can be issued; otherwise, it must have been decided by a court, the LVT, or an independent arbitrator that the leaseholder is in breach. Moreover, the breach of the lease specified in the section 146 notice must have occurred during the twelve years preceding the notice. For breaches older than this, no valid section 146 notice can be served and so forfeiture is not available. If the notice is not complied with, the freeholder may proceed to forfeit; but the leaseholder may go to court for relief from forfeiture. In practice, courts have generally been willing to grant relief, but they cannot do so unless it is formally applied for. If the leaseholder, perhaps failing to realise the seriousness of the situation, fails to go to court and seek relief, the forfeiture will go ahead. If the freeholder breaches the lease, the leaseholder can go to court and seek an order requiring the freeholder to remedy the breach, to pay damages, or to do both. The commonest type of breach complained of by leaseholders is failure to carry out repairs, and this explains why action by leaseholders is less usual; they know that if they force the freeholder to do repairs the costs will be recovered through service charges. Legal action may be the best course if the dispute affects a single leaseholder; but if a number of leaseholders are involved they may well prefer to get rid of the freeholder altogether by collectively enfranchising their leases.

16

Owner Occupiers and Service Charges

The Role of Service Charges

By far the commonest cause of dispute between leaseholders and freeholders is the provision of services and, especially, the levying of service charges. In extreme cases, leaseholders have been asked to contribute thousands of pounds towards the cost of major repairs, and have even suffered forfeiture of the lease if they are unable, or unwilling, to comply. Happily, such instances are rare; but even where the service charges are more moderate, they are often resented by leaseholders. The purpose of this Chapter is to explain the legitimate purpose of service charges and the legal obligations of both the leaseholder and the freeholder, and to offer some warnings about the circumstances where very high service charges are likely to be found.

The difference between long leases and tenancies (short-term and periodic) was set out earlier. One of its most important consequences is that services are paid for in a very different way. In a periodic or short-term tenancy, all the basic costs of providing and managing the housing are paid out of the rent. It is true that there will sometimes be a service charge as well, but it normally covers things such as the provision of heating or communal lighting - things that, however necessary they may be, are peripheral to the central function of providing housing. As a result, service charges in rented property are usually quite moderate and cause little argument.

Contrast the position in leasehold housing. In both types of housing, the landlord is under a legal obligation to the residents to keep the property in good condition and to carry out any work necessary for that purpose; but the landlord of rented property is expected to meet the costs from the rent, whereas the freeholder of leasehold stock has no rent to fall back on (apart from the normally negligible ground rent). How, then, are major costs to be met when they arise? The answer, of course, is from the service charge, which is, therefore, of central importance to the management of leasehold property.

From the freeholder's point of view, the logic of service charges is impeccable. It is perfectly reasonable for freeholders to point out:

- That leaseholders benefit from the work because it has maintained or improved their homes; and
- That the fact that the work has been done means that leaseholders will get a better price when they come to sell; and
- That people that own their homes freehold have to find the money to meet costs of this kind.

To sum up the freeholder's position: the costs have been incurred; the work is for the benefit of the leaseholders; so the leaseholders must pay.

Leaseholders can point out in reply that someone that owns his home freehold can make his own choice when and how to do the repair; he can put up with a slightly leaking roof if he cannot afford to repair it. But freeholders of leasehold property have no such discretion: they are obliged under the lease to do their repairs promptly and if they did not would be liable to legal action by any leaseholder.

So it is difficult for leaseholders to object to the principle of service charges or to ask the freeholder to refrain from carrying out work or to delay it. In short, the purchase of a lease means the acceptance of a commitment to pay the appropriate share of costs.

But does this mean that leaseholders have no scope to challenge or query service charges? No; under sections 18 to 30 of the Landlord and Tenant Act 1985, amended by the 1996 Housing Act and the 2002 Commonhold and Leasehold Reform Act they have extensive legal protection against improper or unreasonable charging by freeholders, and this is discussed later in the Chapter. First, however, we should look at how a typical service charge is made up.

The Components of a Service Charge

The lease will say how often service charges are levied: typically, six-monthly or annually. It is usual to collect the ground rent at the same time, but this is usually a fairly small component of the bill. The service charge proper will normally consist of three elements.

- **The management fee** is the charge made by the freeholder, or the freeholder's agent, to cover the administrative cost of providing the service and collecting the charge. Usually it will be much the same amount from one year to the next, but if major works have occurred the management fee will usually be higher to cover the extra costs of appointing and supervising contractors; 15% of the cost of the works is a common figure.

* **Direct costs (routine expenditure)** cover costs such as the supply of electricity to communal areas, building insurance, and the like. Again, these costs are likely to be fairly constant from year to year, so leaseholders know in advance roughly how much they are likely to have to pay.

* **Direct costs (exceptional expenditure)** cover costs that are likely to be irregular but heavy. They usually result from maintenance and repair, and it is because this component of the service charge is so unpredictable that it gives rise to so many problems. Where a house has been divided into leasehold flats, the freeholder's costs will usually be similar to what a normal home owner would be obliged to pay; in other words, the costs may well be in the thousands (for a new roof, say) but are unlikely to be higher. Even so, a charge of £5000 for a new roof, albeit divided between three or four flats, is still a major cost from the point of view of the individual leaseholder, especially if it is unexpected. The situation can be far worse in blocks of flats, where the costs of essential repair and maintenance may run into millions. Replacement of worn-out lifts, for example, is notoriously costly; and costs arising from structural defects are likely to be higher still. Suppose it costs £2 million to remove asbestos from a block of forty flats: the average cost per flat is £50 000, a figure that may well exceed the value of the individual flats, and is likely to be beyond the reach of most leaseholders. The problem of exceptionally high service charges is looked at in greater detail at the end of the chapter.

Unreasonable Service Charges
a: General Principles

Sections 18 to 30 of the Landlord and Tenant Act 1985, as amended by subsequent legislation, grant substantial protection to leaseholders of residential property. This protection was introduced after complaints of exploitation by unscrupulous leaseholders, who were alleged to be carrying out unnecessary, or even fictitious, repairs at extravagant prices, whilst not providing the information that would have enabled leaseholders to query the bill. The general effect of the Act is to require freeholders to provide leaseholders with full information about service charges and to consult them before expensive works are carried out. It must be stressed, however, that although the Act protects leaseholders against sharp practice by freeholders, and will prevent the recovery of *unreasonable* costs, it will support freeholders, provided they have gone through the necessary formalities described below, in the recovery of their *reasonable* costs, even if those costs are high. To take the example used above of the removal of asbestos from a block of flats: the fact that the average cost per flat is as high as £50 000 does not, in itself, make the charge unreasonable - to make use of the Act, objecting leaseholders have to show, when they are notified that the work is to be carried out (not when the bills arrive), that it was not necessary or could have been carried out cheaper.

A few leases, namely those granted under the right to buy by local authorities or registered housing associations, have some additional protection under the Housing Act 1985 (see below), but sections 18 to 30 apply to all residential leases where the service charge depends on how much the freeholder spends. They set out the key rules that freeholders must observe in order to recover the cost, including overheads, of 'services, repairs or improvements, maintenance or insurance', as well as the freeholder's costs of management. Sections 18 to 30 only apply to service charges, not to other charges such as ground rent.

It should be noted that failure by leaseholders to pay the service charge does not relieve the freeholder of the obligation to provide the services. The freeholder's remedy is to sue the leaseholder for the outstanding charges, or even to seek forfeiture of the lease (see below).

Section 19 of the Act provides the key protection to leaseholders by laying down that service charges are recoverable only if they are 'reasonably incurred' and if the services or works are of a reasonable standard. This means that the charge:

- must relate to some form of service, repair, maintenance, improvement, or insurance that the freeholder is required to provide under the lease;

- must be reasonable (that is, the landlord may not recover costs incurred unnecessarily or extravagantly);

- may cover overheads and management costs only if these too are reasonable.

In addition, the charge must normally be passed on to the leaseholders within 18 months of being incurred, and in some cases the freeholder must consult leaseholders before spending the money. These points are covered below.

The Housing Act 1996 gave leaseholders new powers to refer service charges to the Leasehold Valuation Tribunal (LVT). This is covered below (*Challenging Service Charges*).

b: Consultation with Leaseholders

Section 20 as amended by the 2002 Commonhold and Leasehold Reform Act provides extra protection where the cost of works is more than a certain limit. (£250 or more to the leaseholder). Costs above this level are irrecoverable unless the freeholder has taken steps to inform and consult tenants, although there are a exceptions in special cases (see below). If the leaseholders are not represented by a recognised tenants' association (for which see below) these steps are as follows:

Intention to carry out works: The landlord must write to all leaseholders stating the intention and reasons for carrying out work. There must be a notice period of 30 days.

Estimates At least two estimates must be obtained, of which at least one must be from someone wholly unconnected from the freeholder (obviously a building firm that the freeholder owns or works for is not 'wholly unconnected'; nor is the freeholder's managing agent. Arguably, even a

119

building firm with which the freeholder has no formal connexion could be 'connected' with him if he gives it so much work that it depends on him and is thus subject to his influence)

Notification to leaseholders The freeholder must either display a copy of the estimates somewhere they are likely to be seen by everyone liable to pay the service charges or preferably send copies to everyone liable to pay the charge

Consultation The notification must describe the works to be carried out and must seek comments and observations, giving a deadline for replies and an address in the UK to which they may be sent. The deadline must be at least a month after the notice was sent or displayed.

Freeholder's response The freeholder must 'have regard' to representations received. This does not mean, of course, that the freeholder must do what the leaseholders say. It does mean, however, that the freeholder must consider any comments received, and good freeholders often demonstrate that they have done so by sending a reasoned reply (i.e. not a form letter or bare acknowledgment, but a letter that responds specifically to any points made), even though the Act does not require them to.

It was mentioned above that there are special cases in which these requirements can be set aside. If a service charge is challenged, it is defence for the freeholder to show that the works were so urgent that there was no time for proper consultation. It is also possible for freeholders to enter into long term agreements to carry out works or provide services over a period of years; if so, they must consult before the agreement is entered into but they need not consult separately before each particular element of expenditure under the agreement. Finally, the LVT has a general power to set aside the usual consultation requirements if it seems fair to do so.

Section 20 is important because it gives the leaseholders notification of any unusual items in the offing and gives them an opportunity to raise any concerns and objections. If the leaseholder has any reservations at all, it is vital that they be put before the freeholder at this stage. It is unlikely, in the event of legal action later, that courts or LVTs will support a leaseholder that raised no objection until the bill arrived.

It is surprisingly common for freeholders and their agents to fail to comply with the requirements of section 20. This comment applies not only where the freehold is owned by an individual or a relatively small organisation (where mistakes might be more understandable) but also where the freeholder is a large, well resourced body like a local authority (which should be well able to understand and carry out its legal duties).

As a result leaseholders are often paying service charges that are not due, so all leaseholders should, before paying a service charge containing

unusual items, ensure that section 20, if it applies, has been scrupulously followed. If not, they can refuse to pay.

c: Other Protection for Leaseholders

Grant-aided works: If the freeholder has received a grant towards the cost of carrying out the works, the amount must be deducted from the service charge levied on leaseholders.

Late charging: Service charge bills may not normally include costs incurred more than eighteen months earlier. The freeholder may, however, notify leaseholders within the eighteen month period that they will have to pay a certain cost, and then bill them later. This may happen if, for instance, the freeholder is in dispute with a contractor about the level of a bill or the standard of work.

Pre-charging: Sometimes a lease will contain a provision allowing the freeholder to make a charge to cover future costs besides those already incurred. This practice, which is perfectly lawful in itself, may be in the interests of the leaseholders by spreading over a longer period the cost of major works. It is, however, subject to the same overall requirement of reasonableness.

Court costs: Section 20C provides protection against a specific abuse of the service charge system by freeholders. Previously, freeholders tended to regard their legal costs as part of the process of managing the housing and thus as recoverable from leaseholders. Such an attitude is not necessarily unreasonable: if, for instance, the freeholder is suing a builder for poor work, he is, in effect, acting on behalf of all the leaseholders and it is fair that they should pay any legal costs. But suppose the freeholder were involved in legal proceedings against one of the leaseholders: if the leaseholder lost, he would probably to be ordered to pay the freeholder's costs as well as his own; but if the freeholder lost, and had to pay both his own and the leaseholder's costs, he could simply, under the previous law, recover the money as part of the management element in the service charge. This meant that the freeholder was able to pursue legal action against leaseholders without fear of heavy legal costs in the event of defeat, the very factor that deters most people from too ready a resort to law. To prevent this, section 20C

allows leaseholders to seek an order that the freeholder's legal costs must not be counted towards service charges.

Service charges held on trust: Section 42 of the Landlord and Tenant Act 1987 further strengthened the position of leaseholders by laying down that the freeholder, or the freeholder's agent, must hold service charge monies in a suitable interest-bearing trust fund that will ensure that the money is protected and cannot be seized by the freeholder's creditors if the freeholder goes bankrupt or into liquidation. However, public sector freeholders, notably local authorities and registered housing associations, are exempt from this requirement.

Administration charges: These are the freeholder's costs incurred in complying with leaseholders' requests for information and approvals under the terms of the lease. All such charges must be reasonable. Any demand for administration charges must be accompanied by a summary of leaseholders' rights and obligations in relation to them. The LVT has the power to decide whether or not an administration charge is payable, and if so, to whom and by whom together with the amount, date payable and the manner in which it is paid.

Ground rent: Strictly, this is not part of the service charge but as it is usually collected along with it, it is covered here. It will be specified in the lease and is usually a fairly modest annual sum in the order of £50 or £100. Leaseholders should note that, unlike the service charge and most other charges, the ground rent is not intended to compensate the freeholder for any costs or trouble; it is simply a payment by which the leaseholder recognises that ultimately the property belongs to the freeholder. Therefore freeholders are under no obligation to demonstrate that it is reasonable. But it is not payable unless the landlord has issued a formal request for it, which must specify the amount of the payment, the date on which the leaseholder is liable to pay it and the date (if different) on which it would have been payable under the lease. The date for payment must be at least 30 days and not more than 60 days after the date of the notice.

Insurance: Usually, any insurance required under the lease will be taken out by the freeholder and this is discussed below. Occasionally, however, the leaseholder will be required to take out insurance with a company nominated by the freeholder. If the leaseholder thinks he is getting a poor deal, he can apply to the county court or a Leasehold Valuation Tribunal which, if satisfied that the insurance is unsatisfactory or the premiums are unreasonably high, can order the freeholder to nominate another insurer.

'Period of Grace': When a dwelling is sold under the right to buy by a local authority or non-charitable housing association, the purchaser is given an estimate of service charges for the following five years. This estimate is the maximum recoverable during that time. Some purchasers under the right to buy have, however, had a very rude shock when the five year period of grace expires - see *Exceptionally High Service Charges* below.

d: The role of a recognised tenants' association

The tenants who are liable to pay for the provision of services may, if they wish, form a recognised tenants' association (RTA) under section 29 of the Landlord and Tenant Act 1985. Note that leaseholders count as tenants for this purpose (see Chapter One, where it explained that legally the two terms are interchangeable). If the freeholder refuses to give a notice recognising the RTA, it may apply for recognition to any member of the local Rent Assessment Committee panel ('Rent Assessment Committee' is the official term for a Leasehold Valuation Tribunal when it is carrying out certain functions, not otherwise relevant to leaseholders, under the Rent Act 1977).

An important benefit of having a RTA is that it has the right, at the beginning of the consultation process, to recommend persons or organisations that should be invited to submit estimates. However, the freeholder is under no obligation to accept these recommendations.

Another advantage is that the RTA can, whether the freeholder likes it or not, appoint a qualified surveyor to advise on matters relating to service charges. The surveyor has extensive rights to inspect the freeholder's documentation and take copies, and can enforce these rights in court if necessary.

Against these benefits must be set the principal disadvantage of having a RTA, namely that it weakens the freeholder's obligation to consult individual leaseholders. Where there is a RTA, the freeholder, instead of having to supply copies of the estimates to all leaseholders (or place copies where they are likely to be seen), merely has to send them to the secretary of the RTA, and the individual leaseholders must make do with summaries. Leaseholders - and for that matter, ordinary periodic tenants - should therefore weigh carefully the advantages and disadvantages of setting up a RTA. If they decide against, there is nothing to prevent them from forming an *unrecognised* tenants' (or leaseholders') association, which can represent their interests to the freeholder, provided that it is made clear that formal recognition under section 29 is not being sought.

Challenging Service Charges

The Landlord and Tenant Act not only allows leaseholders to take action against unreasonable behaviour by the freeholder; it also enables them to take the initiative. This is done in two ways: by giving leaseholders rights to demand information, and by allowing them to challenge the reasonableness of the charge.

Any demand for service charges must include details about leaseholders' rights and how they can challenge the charges. If this is not done the leaseholder may withhold payment without penalty.

a: *Right to information*

Freeholders must provide a written summary of costs counting towards the service charge. It must be sent to the leaseholder within six months of the end of the period it covers. The service charge need not be paid until the summary is provided.

The law lays down some minimum requirements for the summary. It must:
- cover all the costs incurred during the twelve months it covers, even if they were included in service charge bills of an earlier or later period (see above for late charging and pre-charging);
- show how the costs incurred by the freeholder are reflected in the service charges paid, or to be paid, by leaseholders;
- say whether it includes any work covered by a grant (see above);
- distinguish: (a) those costs incurred for which the freeholder was not billed during the period; (b) those for which he was billed and did not pay; (c) those for which he paid bills.

If it covers five or more dwellings, the summary must, in addition, be certified by a qualified accountant as being a fair summary, complying with the Act, and supported by appropriate documentation. The purpose of these rules is to put leaseholders in a position to challenge their service charges. After receiving the summary, the leaseholder has six months in which to ask the freeholder to make facilities available so that he can inspect the documents supporting the summary (bills, receipts, and so on) and take copies or extracts. The freeholder must make the facilities available within 21 days after such a request; the inspection itself must be free, although the freeholder can make a reasonable charge for the copies and extracts. Failure to provide these facilities, like failure to supply the summary, is punishable by a fine of up to £2500.

Very similar rules apply where the lease allows, or requires, the freeholder to take out insurance against certain contingencies, such as major repair, and to recover the premiums through the service charge. This is not unreasonable in itself and will, indeed, often be in the interests of leaseholders. The danger is, however, that the freeholder, knowing that the premiums are, in effect, being paid by someone else, has no incentive to shop around for the best deal. Section 30A of the Landlord and Tenant Act 1985 therefore lays down that leaseholders, or the secretary of the recognised tenants' association if there is one, may ask the freeholder for information about the policy. Failure to supply it, or to make facilities to inspect relevant documents available if requested to do so, is an offence incurring a fine of up to £2500.

It must be acknowledged that the rules allowing leaseholders to require information about service charges are, particularly in view of the £2500 fines, fairly onerous from the freeholder's point of view. It is the purpose of this book to inform leaseholders of their rights, not to make life difficult for freeholders: nevertheless, it must be admitted that if leaseholders wish to pursue a policy of confronting freeholders, and to cause them as much trouble as possible, sections 21, 22, and 30A offer plenty of scope.

b: Challenging a service charge

Any leaseholder liable to pay a service charge, and for that matter any freeholder levying one, may refer the charge to a Leasehold Valuation Tribunal to determine its reasonableness. This may be done at any time, even when the service in question is merely a proposal by the freeholder (for instance, for future major works). But the LVT will not consider a service charge if:
-       it has already been approved by a court; or
-       if the leaseholder has agreed to refer it to arbitration; or
-       if the leaseholder has agreed it.

The first of these exceptions is obvious and the second is unlikely to apply very often. The third one is the problem: leaseholders should be careful, in their dealings with freeholders, to say or do nothing that could be taken to imply that they agree with any service charge that is in any way doubtful.

The LVT will consider:

-       whether a service charge is payable and if so when, how, and by whom;
-       whether the freeholder's costs of services, repairs, maintenance, insurance, or management are reasonably incurred;
-       whether the services or works are of a reasonable standard; and
-       whether any payment required in advance is reasonable.

The fees for application to a LVT can be obtained from the LVT and will usually change annually. Appeal against a LVT decision is not to the courts but to the Lands Tribunal.

By section 19 of the Landlord and Tenant Act 1985, any service charge deemed unreasonable by the LVT is irrecoverable by the freeholder. The determination of service charges by the LVT also plays an important part in the rules governing the use of forfeiture to recover service charges. It is to this that we now turn.

Forfeiture for Unpaid Service Charges

Forfeiture was mentioned at the end of Chapter Two. Briefly, it is the right of the freeholder to resume possession of the property if the leaseholder breaches the lease.

By section 81 of the Housing Act 1996, forfeiture for an unpaid service charge is available to the freeholder only if:

- the leaseholder has agreed the charge; or
- the charge has been upheld through post-dispute arbitration or by the Leasehold Valuation Tribunal or a court.

Regarding the first of these, it is necessary only to reiterate the warning to leaseholders to say or do nothing that could possibly be construed as representing their agreement to any service charge about whose legitimacy they have the slightest doubt.

Regarding the second, it should be noted that where the leaseholder has not agreed the service charge, proceedings before the LVT or a court or post-dispute arbitration are necessary before the freeholder can forfeit the lease.

A further requirement is that the amount of money involved must either exceed a certain amount or have been outstanding for a minimum period of time. The Government will set these limits by order. It is currently proposed that the minimum amount will be £350 and the minimum period three years, but this is yet to be confirmed. Note that it is necessary for only one of the requirements to be satisfied.

To sum up, before the leaseholder can forfeit:
- it must have been formally decided that the service charge is due,

- the amount must exceed the minimum amount or have been owed for the minimum time, and
- a section 146 notice must have been served (but this requirement does not apply if the service charge is reserved as rent).

The freeholder can still begin the process by issuing a section 146 notice (see Chapter Two) but it must state that the forfeiture cannot proceed until the requirements of section 81 have been met.

It remains to be seen how these new provisions will operate in practice. Their purpose is to prevent freeholders from using the draconian threat of forfeiture to pressurise leaseholders into paying disputed service charges, and to this extent the position of leaseholders has been greatly strengthened. The danger is that freeholders may respond by getting disputed charges before the LVT as quickly as possible so that forfeiture becomes available if the charges are upheld. Another concern is that some leaseholders, faced with service charges they are unwilling to pay but about which there is no dispute, may be unable to resist the temptation to invent spurious grounds for objection in order to deprive the freeholder of the weapon of forfeiture; this tactic is likely to provoke even relatively easy-going freeholders into legal action.

Once the leaseholder has agreed the service charge or it has been upheld by the LVT or a court or through arbitration, forfeiture becomes a serious threat and in this situation the advice can only be to pay the charge if at all possible. If, however, the leaseholder is unable to pay he may find it helpful to contact his mortgagee (if any). For the mortgagee, forfeiture is a disaster because it is likely to be left with a large unsecured debt on its hands, so many mortgagees in this situation will pay the service charges and add the cost to the outstanding mortgage. This does not solve the leaseholder's long term problem - that his lease commits him to payments he is unable to meet - but it will give him a little breathing space and may enable him to sell up and pay off his debts.

Some leaseholders, especially those of longer standing, may be living on fixed incomes and have very little cash to spare, even though their property is quite valuable. Sometimes their mortgage has been paid off altogether; even if it is still outstanding, it will probably be very small in relation to the value of the property. Leaseholders that find themselves in this 'propertyrich, cash-poor' situation may find it helpful to look at equity release schemes, operated by a number of financial institutions.

Exceptionally High Service Charges

So far this Chapter has focused on service charges of normal proportions that, however unforeseen and unwelcome they may be, should be within the means of the great majority of leaseholders. A minority of leaseholders, however, face the much more serious problem of consistently very high service charges. Where the cause is sharp practice by the freeholder, or failure to observe the legal requirements, the leaseholder can look for protection to the Landlord and Tenant Act as described above. Often, however, the freeholder is not to blame: rather, the problem is that the work is genuinely necessary and unavoidably expensive. In this situation, and provided the landlord carefully follows the procedures laid down, the Landlord and Tenant Act offers no protection.

In what sort of housing is this most likely to occur? It is more likely to affect flats than houses because flats tend to contain potentially very expensive components such as lifts or communal arrangements for heating or ventilation. They are also more likely to have been built using construction methods or designs in vogue at one time but since found to lead to serious maintenance problems and high costs, whereas house building seems to be innately conservative and resistant to innovation: for instance, many blocks of flats contain asbestos, but very few houses.

All these problems apply to flats in general, but there is an additional problem with blocks of flats owned by local authorities and housing associations: namely that, unlike blocks of flats developed by commercial owners for sale, they are likely to combine rented properties, let to periodic tenants in the usual way, with leasehold properties, sold at some point in the past under the right to buy or some similar scheme. These 'mixed managed' blocks present special problems for both categories of resident as well as the freeholder.

Clearly, there is no satisfactory way to resolve this problem. In a privately developed block, occupied wholly by leaseholders, the freeholder might possibly be prevailed upon to delay the repairs for a time if the leaseholders are prepared to put up with the poor conditions; but the Council can hardly be expected to take the same view when most of the residents are periodic tenants. Both the Council and the periodic tenants are likely to argue that the leaseholders are being asked to do no more than they agreed to do when they bought their leases.

In most cases, however, Councils will be able to say, quite truthfully, that they had no idea of the problem when the sale took place, in which case the court is likely to apply the established legal principle of *caveat emptor* - 'let the buyer beware'.

All this book can do is warn prospective leaseholders of the serious problems that can arise in a minority of cases, and suggest some of the questions that they should ask before signing the lease.

1   **What is the condition of the building as a whole?** No one would buy a house, or an individual flat, without looking closely at its condition and estimating how much money it may need to have spent on it. But, when a flat is being bought, whether it is purpose-built or a conversion, it is equally important to look at the entire building of which it forms a part. The vendor should be asked for copies of past service charges, the freeholder should be asked whether major work is likely in the foreseeable future and what it is likely to cost, and an independent surveyor should be asked to report.

2   **What is the leaseholder's liability?** The lease will specify what the leaseholder must pay for. Sometimes it will require him to contribute to things from which he does not benefit. For example, it is common for even ground floor leaseholders to be expected to contribute to the costs of the lifts; and some leaseholders, having paid out of their own pockets to replace their windows, are outraged to discover, when the freeholder has the windows of the whole block renewed, that they are required to pay a share of the cost. Provisions such as these are much resented by many leaseholders, who argue that they are unfair; but the time to object to such unfairness is before signing the lease, not many years later when the bills come in. It is therefore essential that anyone proposing to enter into a lease should first consult a solicitor.

3   **Is there a 'period of grace' or other safeguard?** Right to buy leases contain an estimate of service charges for five years following the sale

and that is the maximum that the Council may charge. Many purchasers, reassured by this, have signed the lease without paying much attention to the likely level of service charges thereafter, expecting perhaps to have sold at a profit and moved on before the five years expire. If so, they have been reminded of what many people forgot during the 1980s: that property prices can go down as well as up. In short, it is unwise to rely on a 'period of grace' to provide anything other than short-term relief; and in particular it is unwise to speculate on the future behaviour of the housing market.

4 **What are the prospects for resale?** Traditionally, the homeowner's last resort in the face of overwhelming financial problems is to sell up in the expectation that the proceeds will suffice to pay off the mortgage, settle other outstanding debts such as service charges, and still leave something over. The stagnant property market of the early 1990s upset many calculations of this kind, but the much stronger market of recent years means that mortgages are often appreciably less than the value of the property, so for many people selling up offers a way out. So it is important to assess the salability of the dwelling by asking whether future purchasers are likely to be put off by anything about the flat itself or the block and district to which it belongs, and above all whether mortgage lenders are likely to look on it favourably.

17

Buying a Freehold and Extending a Lease

LEASEHOLD REFORM, HOUSING AND URBAN DEVELOPMENT ACT 1993

The area of leasehold enfranchisement has attracted a plethora of media and academic interest since its formal introduction in 1967 and has been amended and expanded over the past four decades. The right of long leaseholders to buy their landlord's interest outright or acquire an extended lease term, is unique to England and Wales and, perhaps unsurprisingly, has led to a number of legal challenges over the years. Landlords and tenants alike are anxious to protect their respective property interests in a market that shows no sign of abating. Consequently, this area of the law is continually evolving.

In general terms, the legislation confers two distinct rights: to purchase the freehold, either individually in relation to leasehold houses, or collectively for a block of flats, or to seek a lease extension. Although these rights are curtailed by the statutory tests for qualification, changes to the legislation, introduced by the Commonhold and Leasehold Reform Act 2002, have made it easier than ever for leaseholders to make a claim.

The requirement that leaseholders must have occupied the property in question for a period of two years (the so-called residence requirement) has largely been swept away and replaced by a new, two year ownership test. Indeed, in the case of a collective enfranchisement, even the ownership requirement has been removed. Likewise, qualification tests based on the property's ratable values and rent have gone, with the result that higher value houses, for example, may now enfranchise.

The Collective Right to enfranchise
What is it?

This gives the right for tenants of flats acting together to purchase the freehold and any headleases of their building. In order for the building to qualify under the Act, it must:

• be an independent building or be a part of a building which is capable of independent development; and
• contain two or more flats held by qualifying tenants; and
• have at least two thirds of the flats held by qualifying tenants.

In order to be a qualifying tenant you must have a long lease which means a lease which, when originally granted, was for a term of more than 21 years. However, you must not own three or more flats in the building. You cannot be a qualifying tenant if you hold a business lease.

Notwithstanding the above, the building will not qualify if:
• it comprises four or less units and has a "resident freeholder";
• more than 25% of the internal floor space (excluding common parts) is used for non-residential purposes;
• the building is part of an operational railway.

How do I prepare for a claim?

Any qualifying tenant can give a notice to his landlord or the managing agent requiring details of the various legal interests in the block. This notice places no commitment on the tenant but the response to the notice should provide the tenant with the information necessary for him to ascertain whether the building contains a sufficient number of qualifying tenants for it to qualify.

Having established that the building qualifies, it is then advisable to ascertain whether you have a sufficient number of tenants who want to participate, both for the purpose of qualifying for enfranchisement and for the purpose of being able to finance the acquisition. In order to qualify for enfranchisement, you need to establish that the number of participating tenants comprises not less than one half of all the flats in the building. However, if there are only two flats in the building then both must participate.

When you have established that the building qualifies and that there is a sufficient number of qualifying tenants who wish to participate, then there are five further practical steps which should be taken before embarking on the enfranchisement procedure.

First, you need to establish what it is going to cost by obtaining a valuation. In simple terms, the price to be paid by the participating tenants to purchase the freehold of the building is the aggregate of:

- The building's investment value to the freeholder-the capitalised value of his ground rents and the value of his reversion (being the present freehold vacant possession value deferred for the unexpired term of the lease).

- One half of the marriage value-the increased value attributable to the freehold by virtue of the participating tenants being able to grant themselves extended leases at nil premium and a peppercorn rent. The marriage value attributable to a lease held by a participating tenant will be deemed to be nil if that lease has an unexpired term of more than 80 years at the date that the initial notice is given.

- Compensation for loss of value of other property owned by the freeholder, including development value consequent to the severance of the building from that other property.

The valuation date is the date that the claim notice is given. Value added to the flat of a participating tenant by tenant's improvements is disregarded in the valuation.

For the purposes of calculating price, the tenants should take the advice of a properly qualified surveyor or valuer with experience in the field of enfranchisement and knowledge of the market.

In addition to the price and the participating tenants' own legal costs and valuation fees, the claimants will be required to reimburse the freeholder his legal costs and valuation fees.

Secondly, the participators will need to establish how to finance the cost of acquisition. It may, for example, be necessary for a number of participating tenants to seek a further advance from a Building Society or Bank. In particular, the participators will want to decide who is to finance the purchase of the non-participators' flats and on what basis.

Thirdly, it will be necessary to establish what vehicle the participating tenants should use in order to buy the freehold and how they will establish and regulate the relationship between themselves. In most cases, this is likely to be through a company structure, although in some circumstances a trust might be more appropriate. It should be noted that the participating tenants do not all have to have equal shares, so that the proportion of the shareholdings will be a matter for negotiation between them.

The 2002 Act provides for collective claims to be made through the mechanism of a Right to Enfranchise (RTE) company. However those provisions have never been brought into force and it is unlikely that they will be.

Fourthly, the participating tenants should seek advice to establish whether there are tax implications to the transaction, both in relation to their individual positions and in relation to the vehicle chosen to buy the freehold.

Finally, the collective enfranchisement legislation provides no guidance or controls on the way in which the participating tenants should work together in order to acquire the freehold. Since the purchase may well involve substantial sums of money and is likely to take time to complete and, during this time, the participating tenants will be heavily reliant on each other for the performance of tasks within strict limits, it is strongly advised that, before embarking on a claim, the participating tenants should enter into a formal agreement (called a participation agreement) in order to regulate the relationship between them during the course of the claim.

How is the claim made?

It is important to be aware that most of the time limits imposed on the procedural stages of the claim are strict and a failure to do something within the required time frame can have dire consequences for the defaulter. It is therefore essential that, by the time you reach the next stage of the procedure, you are well organised and backed by expert professional advice.

The reason for this is that the next procedural step is the service by the participating tenants on the landlord of what the Act calls the initial notice – the notice which claims the right to collective enfranchisement. Costs start to run against the tenants from the time they serve the initial notice. Amongst other things this notice must specify:

- the extent of the property to be acquired – supported by a plan;
- full particulars of all the qualifying tenants in the building –
not just the participating tenants;
- the price being offered for the freehold – the offer should be genuine;

135

• the name and address of the nominee purchaser – the person or company nominated by the participating tenants to conduct the negotiations and to buy the freehold on their behalf;
• the date by which the freeholder must give his counter-notice, being a date not less than two months from the date of the service of the initial notice.

The freeholder is likely to respond with a procedural notice requiring the participating tenants to deduce title. The freeholder's valuer is also likely to inspect the building for the purpose of carrying out a valuation.

Within the period specified in the initial notice, the freeholder must serve his counter-notice. First and foremost, this must state whether or not the claim is admitted. If it is not, then the participating tenants must decide if they wish to dispute the rejection through the courts.

There are circumstances where the freeholder can resist a claim on the ground of redevelopment.

If the claim is admitted, then the counter-notice must state, amongst other things:

• which of the proposals contained in the initial notice are acceptable;
• which of the proposals contained in the initial notice are not acceptable and what are the freeholder's counter-proposals –particularly on price;
• whether the freeholder wants a leaseback on any units in the building not held by a qualifying tenant (for example, a flat subject to a short term tenancy or a commercial unit).
• compensation for loss in value of other property owned by the freeholder, including development value consequent to sale

Disputes

If any terms of acquisition (including the price) remain in dispute after two months following the date of the counter-notice, then either party can apply to the leasehold valuation tribunal for the matter in dispute to be determined.

This application must be made within six months following the date of the counter-notice or the claim is lost. Most claims are settled by negotiation. If a leasehold valuation tribunal is required to make a determination, then there is a right to appeal that decision to the Lands Tribunal if permission is given to do so.

Completion

Once the terms of acquisition have been agreed or determined by the leasehold valuation tribunal, then the matter reverts to a conveyancing transaction with the parties entering into a sale contract on the terms agreed or determined and thence to completion.

If the matter proceeds to completion, then the participating tenants, through their nominee purchaser, will become the freeholder of the building, subject to the various flat leases. In effect, the participating tenants will replace the existing freeholder. This will put them in a position to grant themselves extended leases.

There may be taxation consequences on granting an extended lease, particularly for second home owners. There will also be responsibilities. The participating tenants will become responsible for the management of the building and the administration of the service charge account in accordance with the covenants in the original leases.

If the nominee purchaser is a company, all participators will be shareholders and some will be officers of that company. These are all matters on which clear professional advice will be needed. It is important to note that an individual tenant has no right to become
a participating tenant – even if he is a qualifying tenant. It is a matter for the tenants to resolve between themselves. You can always ask to be allowed to join in, but you will have no remedy if refused. If a group does form without you – and does not need you – you may well find yourself left out.

However, if you are left out, that need not necessarily be the end of the road. This is because of the second major innovation that was introduced by the 1993 Act – the individual right to acquire a new lease.

The individual right to extend leases
What is it?

The individual right to a statutory lease extension applies to all qualifying tenants of flats. The condition is that you must be the tenant of a flat which you hold on a long lease (i.e. a lease for an original term in excess of 21 years). Furthermore, you must have owned the lease for at least two years before the date of the claim. For the purpose of the lease extension, There is no limit to the number of flats you may own in the building and you may extend any or all of them provided that the conditions are met. However, you cannot be a qualifying tenant if you hold a business lease.

Prior to the 2002 Act, the personal representatives of a deceased tenant had no rights to make a claim, even where the deceased tenant was able to fulfil the qualifying conditions. However, such personal representatives can now make a claim provided that the right is exercised within a period of two years from the date of grant of probate.

What do I get?

If you qualify, then you will be entitled to acquire a new extended lease in substitution for your existing lease. This extended lease will be for a term expiring 90 years after the end of the current lease and will reserve a peppercorn rent throughout the term.

Broadly, the lease will otherwise be on the same terms as the existing lease but the landlord will have certain additional redevelopment rights, exercisable within 12 months before the expiration of the current lease term and within 5 years before the expiration of the extended lease.

The price

The price to be paid for the new lease will be the aggregate of:
• the diminution in value of the landlord's interest in the flat, consequent on the grant of the extended lease; being the capitalised value of the landlord's ground rent and the value of his reversion (being the present near-freehold vacant possession value deferred for the unexpired lease term);

• 50% of the marriage value (the additional value released by the tenant's ability to merge the extended lease with the existing lease) must be paid to the landlord although the marriage value will be deemed to be nil if the existing lease has an unexpired term of more than 80 years at the date of the claim;
• compensation for loss in value of other property owned by the freeholder, including development value, consequent on the grant of the new lease

The valuation date is the date of the claim notice. In addition to the price and the tenant's own legal costs and valuation fees, you will also be required to reimburse the freeholder his legal costs and valuation fees.

How do I claim?

The procedure to be followed is very similar to that for collective enfranchisement. It is therefore important to be aware that most of the time limits imposed on the procedural stages of the claim are strict and a failure to do something within the required time frame can have dire consequences for the defaulter.

The qualifying tenant can serve a preliminary notice to obtain information. Thereafter, he serves his notice of claim (in this case called the tenant's notice of claim) which amongst other things needs to state:

• a description of the flat – but not necessarily with a plan;
• sufficient particulars to establish that the lease qualifies;
• the premium being offered – it must be a bona fide offer;
• the terms of the new lease;
• the date by which the landlord must give the counter-notice, being a date not less than two months from the date of service of the tenant's notice.

The landlord is likely to respond with a procedural notice requiring payment of a deposit (equal to 10% of the premium being offered) and asking the tenant to deduce title. The landlord's valuer is also likely to inspect the flat for the purpose of carrying out a valuation.

Within the period specified in the tenant's notice, the landlord must serve his counter-notice. First and foremost, this must state whether or not the claim is admitted. If it is not, then the tenant must decide if he wishes to dispute the rejection through the courts. However, unlike a collective enfranchisement claim where the nominee purchaser makes the application to the court in these circumstances, in the case of the statutory lease extension, it is the landlord who makes the application if he has refused the claim.

Enfranchisement

There are circumstances where the landlord can resist a claim on the ground of redevelopment. If the claim is admitted, then the counter-notice must state, amongst
other things:

• which of the proposals contained in the tenant's notice are acceptable;
• which of the proposals contained in the tenant's notice are not
acceptable and what are the landlord's counter-proposals – particularly the premium.

Disputes

If either the terms of the lease or the premium remain in dispute after two months following the date of the counter-notice, then either party can apply to the leasehold valuation tribunal for the matter in dispute to be determined.

This application must be made within six months following the date of the counter-notice or the claim is lost. Most claims are settled by negotiation. If a leasehold valuation tribunal
is required to make a determination, then there is a right to appeal that decision to the Lands Tribunal if permission is given to do so

Completion

Once the terms of the lease and the premium have been agreed or determined by the leasehold valuation tribunal, then the matter reverts to a conveyancing transaction with the parties proceeding to completion of the new lease.

The tenant can withdraw at any time and there are provisions for the tenant's notice to be considered withdrawn if certain strict time limits are not met by the tenant. As in collective enfranchisement, the tenant is on risk as to costs as from the date of his tenant's notice so it is essential to be prepared and to be properly advised before starting down the road to an extension.

A tenant's notice is capable of being assigned but only in conjunction with a contemporaneous assignment of the lease. It is common for a seller to serve a notice and then sell that notice with the lease to a purchaser, who will take over the claim. There is no limit to the number of times that a tenant can exercise this right – so long as he is prepared to pay the costs for doing so.

Enfranchisement of Houses-Leasehold Reform Act 1967
What is the right?

The Leasehold Reform Act 1967 gives the tenant of a leasehold house who fulfils certain rules of qualification the right to acquire the freehold and any intermediate leases.

How do I qualify?

In looking at the rules of qualification under the 1967 Act, there are three basic questions that need to be answered. First, does the building qualify. Secondly, does the lease qualify. Thirdly, does the tenant qualify. In order for the building to qualify, it must be a 'house'. This has developed a wide definition and can mean a shop with a flat above, or a building converted to flats. However, one essential feature is that there must be no material over or under-hang with an adjoining building (if there is, then it is likely to be a flat).

The lease must comprise the whole of the house and it must be a long tenancy, i.e., a lease with an original term of more than 21 years. However, if it is a business tenancy, then it will not qualify if it is for an original term of 35 years or less.

The tenant must have owned the lease of the house for a period of at least two years before the date of the claim. Prior to the 2002 Act, it was also necessary for the tenant to occupy the house as his only or main residence for a three year period. The residence test has now been abolished save in limited circumstances.

If a house is mixed use so that there is a business tenancy (for example a building comprising a shop with a flat above) or if the house includes a flat which is subject to a qualifying lease under the 1993 Act (see above), then the tenant is still required to fulfil a residence test. However, it is modified so that the tenant has to occupy the house as his only or main residence only for two years or periods amounting in aggregate to two years in the preceding ten years.

Prior to the 2002 Act, the personal representatives of a deceased tenant had no right to make a claim., even where the deceased tenant was able to fulfill the qualifying conditions. However, such personal representatives can now make a claim provided that the right is exercised within a period of two years from the date of grant of probate.

The Price

The 1967 Act has three different valuation methods. In every case, the valuation date is the date of the claim.

If the house qualified pre-1933 (i.e. by not needing to rely on amendments made to the financial limits and/or low rent conditions by either the 1933 Act, the 1996 Act or the 2002 Act) and had a ratable value of less than £1,000 (£500 outside the Greater London Area) on 31st March 1990 then the valuation is under section 9(1). This section expressly excludes any marriage value and restricts the value to a proportion of the site value.

If the house qualifies pre-1933 but did not have a ratable value of less than £1,000 (£500 outside the Greater London Area) on 31st March 1990, the valuation is under section 9 (1A). The valuation elements here are:

- The capitalised value of the landlords ground rent and the value of his reversion (being the present freehold vacant possession value deferred for the unexpired lease term; and
- 50% of the marriage value (the additional value released by the tenants ability to merge the freehold and leasehold interests) must be to the landlord although the marriage value will be deemed to be nil if the lease has an unexpired term of more than 80 years at the date of the claim.

If the house qualifies post-1933 (i.e. the claimant needs to rely on amendments made to the financial limits/low rent conditions by either the 1933 Act or the 2002 Act) then the valuation is under section 9 (1C). This is broadly the same as section 9(1A) valuation except that the freeholder can be compensated for loss in value of other property owned by him, including development value, consequent on the severance of the house from the other property.

How do I claim?

The procedure for a claim is relatively straightforward. The tenant serves his notice of claim, which is in prescribed form and needs to state (inter alia):

• a description of the house – but not necessarily with a plan;
• particulars to establish that the lease and tenant qualify;
• what the tenant thinks is the basis of valuation.

In addition to the price and the tenant's own legal costs and valuation fees, he will be required to reimburse the freeholder his legal costs and valuations fees. The landlord is likely to respond with a procedural notice requiring payment of a deposit (equal to three times the rent payable under the lease) and asking the tenant to deduce title and (if a residence test is relevant) to produce evidence by statutory declaration that he fulfils the residence condition.

The landlord's valuer is also likely to inspect the house for the purpose of carrying out a valuation. The Act requires the landlord to state, within two months of the notice of claim being served, whether or not he admits the claim. If the claim is not admitted then the tenant must decide if he wishes to dispute the rejection through the courts. A freeholder cannot resist a claim on redevelopment grounds.

Disputes9(1C). This is broadly tame as a valuation

If the claim is admitted and either the terms of the conveyance or the price remain in dispute after two months following the date of the notice of claim, then either party can apply to the leasehold valuation tribunal for the matter in dispute to be determined. There are no time limits on the making of this application.

Completion

Once the terms of the conveyance and the purchase price have been agreed or determined by the leasehold valuation tribunal, the matter reverts to a conveyancing transaction with the parties proceeding to completion.

The tenant can withdraw at any time up to one month following the determination of the purchase price. Unlike collective enfranchisement and statutory lease extension claims, there are no strict procedural time limits. However, the tenant is liable for the landlord's costs as from the date of his notice of claim.

The extended lease option

The 1967 Act also allows the qualifying tenant of a house to take an extended lease of the house for a term of 50 years to expire after the term date of the existing lease at a modern ground rent throughout the extended term and without payment of a premium. This right has been little exercised in recent years not least because none of the amendments relating to the abolition of financial limits and the low rent test introduced by the 1993 Act, the 1996 Act and the 2002 Act apply to it. Furthermore, the extended lease originally had no statutory protection and carried no right to acquire the freehold.

However, following the 2002 Act, all tenancies extended under the 1967 Act now have security of tenure. Furthermore, the tenant under an extended lease now has the right to acquire the freehold, if he otherwise fulfils the qualifying conditions; in such cases, the purchase price will be determined in accordance with section 9(1C) but with modified assumptions.

18

RELATIONSHIP BREAKDOWN AND HOUSING RIGHTS

When a relationship breaks down, whether the people in question are married or not, problems can often occur in relation to the property that was home. The rights of people will depend mainly on whether they are married or not, whether there are children involved and the legal status of individuals in the home.

Housing rights in an emergency

In the main, it is women who suffer from domestic violence. This section refers to women but the rights are the same for men.

If you are women and have been threatened by a man and are forced to leave your home then there are several possibilities for action in an emergency. The first of these is either going to a women's refuge. These provide shelter, advice and emotional support for women and children. These refuges will always try to admit you and as a result are sometimes crowded. They will always try to find you somewhere to live in the longer term. Refuges have a 24-hour telephone service if you need to find somewhere. For addresses see *useful addresses* at the back of this book.

Approaching the council

A person suffering domestic violence who has been forced to flee can approach the local council and ask for help as a homeless person. Councils will demand proof of violence and you will need to get evidence from a professional person, such as doctor or social worker or police. The council decides whether or not it has a duty to help you and you should seek advice if they refuse. Some councils, but not all will offer help to battered women. If you are accepted as homeless then the council should not send you back to the area where the violence began.

Obtaining a court order

Another course of action in an emergency is to obtain a court order against the man you live with. Courts can issue orders stating that a man:

- Should not assault you or harass you
- Not to assault any children living with you
- To leave the home and not to return
- To keep a certain distance from your home or any other place where your children go regularly.
- To let you back in your home if you have been excluded.

If you believe a court order would help you should get advice on where to find a solicitor or law centre that deals with these types of applications to the court. Certain orders are harder to get than others, such as exclusion orders. Matters need to be very serious indeed before such an order will be made. However, you will be advised of this when approaching a solicitor or law centre.

Failure to obey the terms and conditions laid down in the order can lead to arrest for contempt and a fine or even imprisonment.

Long term rights to the home

Long term rights to stay in a home depend on a number of circumstances. If you are married and the ownership or tenancy of the property is in joint names you have equal rights to live in the property. If it is owned then you will have a right to a share of the proceeds if it is sold. In certain circumstances have a right to more (or less) than a half share, or to the tenancy in your name after divorce.

If you are married but the ownership or tenancy is in one name only there are laws to protect the rights of the other party. Courts have the power to decide who has the ownership or rights over the matrimonial home, even if the property is held in one persons name only. This can also apply to people who were married but are now divorced and to those who were planning to get married within three years of their engagement.

Spouses who are not the owner or tenant of the home have a right to stay there. The court has the power to exclude either of the spouses, even if they are sole or joint owner or tenant. If your husband has left and stopped paying the rent or mortgage payments, the landlord or building society is obliged to accept payments from you, if you wish to make them, even if the property is not in your name. If the home is owned by your husband then you can register your right to live in it. This prevents your husband selling the home before the court has decided who should live there. And also prevents him taking out a second mortgage on the property without your knowledge. This is known as 'registering a charge' on the home. The court also has the power to transfer a fully protected private tenancy, an assured tenancy or a council or housing association tenancy from one partner to another.

If the matrimonial home is owner occupied and proceedings have started for a divorce, the court will decide how the value of the property will be divided up. The law recognises that, even if the property is in the husbands name only, the wife has a right to a share in its value, that she often makes a large unpaid contribution through housework or looking after children and that this should be recognised in divorce proceedings. The court looks at a number of things when reaching a decision:

- The income and resources of both partners
- The needs of you and your husband
- The standard of living that you and your husband had before the marital breakdown
- Ages of partners and length of marriage
- Contributions to the welfare of the family
- Conduct of partners
- Loss of benefits that you might have had if the marriage had not have broken down.

The court also has to consider whether there is any way that they can make a 'clean break' between you and you husband so that there are no further financial ties between you.

In certain circumstances, the court can order sale of the matrimonial home and the distribution of proceed between partners.

If you are not married

If you are not married then your rights will depend on who is the tenant or the owner of the home.

Tenants

If a tenancy is in joint names then you both have equal rights to the home. You can exclude your partner temporarily as we have seen by a court order. If you are a council tenant then you may want to see if you can get the council to rehouse you. You should get advice on this from an independent agency (see useful addresses).

If the tenancy is in your partners name only then the other person can apply for the right to stay there, for their partner to be excluded or for the tenancy to be transferred.

Home owners

If you live in an owner occupied property you and you partner may have certain rights to a share of the property even if you are not married.

If the home is jointly owned then you have a clear right to a share in its value. If one person has contributed moiré than the other then a court can decide that an equal share is unfair. The court cannot order the transfer of the ownership of property but it can order the sale and distribution of the proceeds.

If the home is in one persons name there is no automatic right to live in the home, even if there are children. However, a solicitor acting on your behalf can argue that by virtue of marriage and contribution you should be allowed to stay there and be entitled to a share.

19

HOUSING ADVICE

General advice

Citizens Advice Bureaus, which are situated throughout the U.K., provide advice on all problems, including housing and other matters such as legal, welfare benefits and relationship breakdown. If appropriate they can refer you for more specialist help to a solicitor or advice agency. This advice is free of charge. To find a local office, look in the telephone directory under National Association of Citizens Advice Bureau.

Housing Advice Centres

In many areas there are specialist advice centres offering housing aid and advice. The service they offer varies from one-off information to detailed help over a long period. There are two main types of housing advice centres, Local council housing aid centres which can advise on all kinds of problems, although they will not be able to take action against their own council. Independent housing aid centres may be better equipped to do this. These centres can offer detailed assistance over a length of time and also one-off advice. There are a number of independent housing aid centres throughout the country operated by Shelter. You should contact Shelter for you're nearest centre.

Other specialist advice

Law centres-they offer free advice and can sometimes represent you in court. They can usually advise on all aspects of law and also advise battered women. They cannot, however, take divorce cases. For this you will need a solicitor. Shelter can provide a list of law centres.

For advice on welfare rights you should try the local council, who may employ a welfare rights advisor. Advisers can also contact the advice line which is run by the Child Poverty Action Group. For women's rights the Women's Aid Federation England and Welsh Women's Aid refer battered women, with or without children, to refuges. They can put you in touch with sympathetic solicitors and local women's aid groups and can offer a range of other advice, such as welfare benefits.

For immigration advice, the Joint Council for the Welfare of Immigrants offers advice on all types of problems connected with immigration and nationality. The United Kingdom Immigrants Advisory Service offers advice and help on problems with immigration. The Refugee Council has an advice service for refugees and asylum seekers.

Advice from solicitors

Solicitors can advise you on all aspects of the law, represent you in certain courts and, if necessary, get a barrister to represent you. It is best to find a solicitor who specialises in housing rights as they usually have a wider knowledge of specific areas. You can get a list of solicitors who specialise in housing law from the Community Legal Service (CLS) Directory in your local library. The list is also on the CLS website. Citizens Advice Bureaus can also supply specialist solicitor details.

Free advice and help

The legal Help Scheme can pay for up to two hours worth of free advice and assistance and for matrimonial cases up to three hours. The scheme is means tested and you must come withy the limits of the scheme to qualify. For details of the scheme you should approach a Citizens Advice Bureau or a solicitors practice operating the scheme. You must have reasonable grounds for defending an action. In certain cases, if you succeed in obtaining cash compensation then you may have to pay a proportion of it back, this is known as the *statutory charge.*

Appendix 1 – Useful addresses

Age UK England
Tavis House
1-6 Tavistock Square
London WC1H 9NA
020 8679 8000
www.ageuk.org.uk

Building Societies Association
6th Floor York House
23 Kingsway
London WC2B 6UJ
020 7520 5900
www.bsa.org.uk

Child Poverty Action Group
94 White Lion Street
London N1 9PF
020 7837 7979

Consumers Association (Which?)
2 Marylebone Road
London NW1 4DF
020 7770 7000
www.which.co.uk

Disability Rights
12 City Forum
250 City Road
London EC1V 8AF
www.disabilityrightsuk.org
0207 250 3222

Equality and Human Rights Commission
www.equalityhumanrights.com
0808 800 0082

London Gay and Lesbian Switchboard
0300 330 0630
www.llgs.org.uk

Homeless Link
Gateway House
Milverton Street
London SE11 4AP
www.homeless.org.uk
0207 840 4430

Immigration Advisory Service
0844 887 0111
www.iasservice.org.uk

Legal Action Group
242 Pentonville Road
London N1 9UN
020 7833 2931

Liberty (formerly national Council for Civil Liberties)
0207 403 3888
www.liberty-human-rights.org.uk

Index

All titles, listed below, in the Straightforward Guides Series can be purchased online, using credit card or other forms of payment by going to www.straightfowardco.co.uk A discount of 25% per title is offered with online purchases.

Law
A Straightforward Guide to:
Consumer Rights
Bankruptcy Insolvency and the Law
Employment Law
Private Tenants Rights
Health and Safety Law
Family law
Small Claims in the County Court
Contract law
Intellectual Property and the law
Divorce and the law
Leaseholders Rights
The Process of Conveyancing
Knowing Your Rights and Using the Courts
Producing Your own Will
Housing Rights
The Bailiff the law and You
Probate and The Law
Company law
What to Expect When You Go to Court
Guide to Competition Law
Give me Your Money-Guide to Effective Debt Collection
Caring for a Disabled Child

General titles
Inheritance Tax-A Guide
Letting Property for Profit
Buying, Selling and Renting property

Buying a Home in England and France
Bookkeeping and Accounts for Small Business
Creative Writing
Freelance Writing
Writing Your own Life Story
Writing performance Poetry
Writing Romantic Fiction
Speech Writing

Teaching Your Child to Read and write
Teaching Your Child to Swim
Raising a Child-The Early Years

Creating a Successful Commercial Website
The Straightforward Business Plan
The Straightforward C.V.
Successful Public Speaking

Handling Bereavement
Play the Game-A Compendium of Rules
Individual and Personal Finance
Understanding Mental Illness
The Two Minute Message
Guide to Self Defence
Buying a Used Car
Tiling for Beginner
Understanding the Stock market

Go to:

www.straightforwardco.co.uk